Carp Fishing

CARP
FISHING

TIM PAISLEY

The Crowood Press

First published in 1988 by
The Crowood Press
Ramsbury, Marlborough,
Wiltshire SN8 2HE

Reprinted 1989 twice

British Library Cataloguing in Publication Data

Paisley, Tim
Carp fishing
1. Carp. Angling – Manuals
I. Title
799.1'752

ISBN 1 85223 119 X

Dedication

**Especially for Tim (Mark II, improved version)
and Suzy Paisley,**

and for those who give more than they take.

Typeset by Chippendale Type, Otley, West Yorkshire.
Printed in Great Britain by
Redwood Burn Limited, Trowbridge, Wiltshire

Contents

Acknowledgements

My warmest thanks to the following friends who took the time and trouble to pass on some of their great knowledge and valuable experience through their lovely written contributions: Greg Fletcher, Bill Cottam, Dave Preston, Vic Cranfield, Ken Townley, Brian Garner, Brian Skoyles.

My grateful thanks to the following for their photographic contributions to this book: Kevin Clifford, Vic Cranfield, Bill Walford, Dave Walker, Bill Cottam, Chris Shelley, Jim Gibbinson, Lenny Middleton, Jack Hilton, Rod Hutchinson, Steve Corbett, Lee Jackson, Alan Smith, Pete Springate, Brian Garner, Ken Townley, Martin Herbertson and the Hampshire Carp Fishers, Brian Skoyles, Jim Fielding, Steve Justice, Julian Cundiff, Dave Preston, Nick Elliott, Greg Fletcher and Baz Griffiths.

My special thanks to Brian Naylor for his magnificent drawings, which were produced under considerable time pressure and, in part, on the basis of some extremely vague directions.

I would also like to acknowledge the considerable influence on my thinking and writing of four great carp fishing pathfinders: Rod Hutchinson, Fred Wilton, Lenny Middleton and the late Dick Walker. Without the lead they have given we would have precious little on which to base our own efforts.

Introduction

How do you start to convey to others what is involved in fishing for and catching carp? Taking carp fishing at its simplest, you can give someone a bait, demonstrate a presentation, detail the necessary tackle and tell him which water to go to, secure in the knowledge that he should catch carp. But is carp fishing that simple? Well, that's part of the problem, because it can be! If you are armed with the right bait, the tackle and the knowledge that is now freely available, the carp in some waters can be comparatively easy to catch.

But, if all carp anglers were interested only in catchable carp from known producing waters, carp fishing would not have acquired its present growing army of devotees who eat, sleep and drink carp fishing. People take up carp fishing for any of a variety of reasons; for those who continue, these fish acquire a mystique of their own. In the mind they represent a challenge. Catching a few catchable carp can diminish the mystique and erode the challenge because at the outset it isn't always obvious that there are carp – and *carp*. Nor is it clear that the main motivation for going carp fishing isn't always the catching of carp. If it was, we would all stick with producing waters where we would be assured of success. No, there is more to it. If angling is an escape, carp fishing is the great escape.

Those carp men who go on carp fishing for longest tend to have two things in common: they enjoy being at the water for long periods and they always see carp fishing as a challenge. When they find that the carp they are fishing for are becoming easy to catch, they move on to a new water where the carp fishing won't seem easy – where the fish represent a new challenge. Because of this need for a fresh challenge, carp fishing tends to be an evolutionary process. You may start out fishing a water where you are hoping to catch six fish in a day and finish up whiling away the years on a water where you will do well to catch six fish in a season.

I was originally asked to write a book about basic carp fishing, but as I can't define basic carp fishing, even to myself, I couldn't realistically attempt the writing of a book about it. If I hadn't been asked I don't think I would have attempted a book of this type, but the more I thought about it the more I liked the idea of putting together some sort of volume which might help carp men catch carp; and catching carp is, I suppose, basic carp fishing. So this is, as the title suggests, a book about fishing for carp. I think it is fairly basic; if you disagree then all I can do is quote Al Jolson and say 'You ain't seen nothing yet'!

I'm a prolific reader and I'm only too well aware of the many excellent books there are about carp fishing. Read as much as you can and try to relate everything of relevance to the waters you are on and the fish you are after. In theory all the information you require to catch carp is contained in the pages that follow. In practise it isn't possible to produce such a book. When it comes down to the nitty-gritty of putting a fish on the bank you have got to do that for yourself, or with a little help from your friends. We cannot give you experience. Everything you read, and do, and think, and talk about connected with carp fishing is part of your experience. Successful carp fishing comes from applying common sense to your accumulated knowledge. Applying common sense means thinking.

Thinking and experience are the basis of success in most things and carp fishing is certainly no exception. Experience you acquire but it begins with the first moment of involvement. 'Expert' is a kindred word to 'experience', though you will be a very rare animal if you become a carp-fishing expert.

Occasionally you may start to think that you have cracked it, particularly if you concentrate your attentions on one water over a period of time. But just when complacency is setting in things start to go wrong and you discover that you are being out-thought – not just by one fish, but by a water full of them. You need some sort of experience on which to base your thinking to get the indicators moving again, even if it's only to the extent of understanding that you've got to start using a different-flavoured shop-bought boilie.

A number of experienced carp-fishing friends from around the country have contributed to the book and I'm grateful to them for their efforts. I'm pleasantly surprised how well their contributions emphasise some of the points I try to make. I asked each contributor to write about the capture of a carp, and we can all learn a great deal from their experiences. Ken Townley even told me which carp he was going to catch! The writings of the contributors appear here because they are all consistent, experienced carp men. They have all caught bigger carp than the ones they pose with within these pages but I

Kevin Clifford, prolific catcher of big fish, with a fine catch taken on sweetcorn in the mid-1970s.

intentionally set a mid-twenties limit on their target fish because in my mind anything over 25lb is a very big fish indeed.

I've based the book on shared experiences because we all fish differently and it is both refreshing and eye-opening to have a variety of methods and thought processes to draw on. I've enjoyed reading the contributors' pieces as they've come in, and I've learned from them. I hope our combined efforts help you to enjoy your carp fishing – and to catch your share of the carp, whether you are just starting or have been at it for over thirty years.

1

Seventy-Five Years of Carp Fishing

'Then the coiled line began to go through the rings, and I realised that here was a bite . . . .'

Words written by Hugh Sheringham following the capture of a Cheshunt carp of 16lb 4oz early this century. The words appeared in Mr Sheringham's book *Coarse Fishing*, and the account of the capture was later reproduced in BB's books *The Fisherman's Bedside Book* and *Confessions of a Carp Fisher*. They were first published seventy-five years ago; carp fishing goes back a long way.

This book is not really concerned with the history of carp fishing, or the timelessness of it, or the magic of it, but it would be a very incomplete volume if it did not convey at least something of all those aspects which help lend a special magic to what is – on paper – a purely technical exercise. Most carp anglers seek far more from carp fishing than the mere catching of carp.

The chapters that follow are concerned mainly with fishing for carp but for the few pages of this chapter I will reflect briefly on what has gone before. This look backwards emphasises that the modern carp-fishing methods are new. Periodically an original thinker will bring about a carp-fishing revolution; in time the revolutionary method becomes the norm and its effectiveness is diminished, or lost. The thinkers are able to think things out for themselves and keep catching by modifying, improvising and compromising between methods old and new – combining thinking with angling ability, hard work and a willingness to experiment.

We have reached an odd situation in the current carp world. Most writers concentrate on writing about modifications to modern methods, with the result that there are now anglers carp fishing who think that there is *a* method of fishing for carp – a bare hook, a heavy lead, a clipped up line and a boiled bait or particle. That *can* be the method, no one can deny it. But it

24 June 1911: Hugh Sheringham at Cheshunt.
'*Then I thrilled to a movement at the other end of the line, which gradually increased until the fish was on the move again . . .*'

24 July 1930: Albert Buckley at Mapperley.
'Owing to the gale with the wind blowing straight towards me down the lake I could only fish about two yards from the embankment.'

BRIAN NAYLOR – 87 ©

wasn't always so and it is becoming increasingly clear that it won't always be so. Times have changed and will continue to do so.

I have asked my friend Brian Naylor to do the impossible and portray through his talented pen impressions of a number of carp captures from the past that have fired my imagination more than others. There is a romance to carp fishing and even in a book that sets out to be informative it is not possible to ignore that feel of mystery and achievement that draws us in pursuit of our quarry. I hope that that feel is generated by these drawings. The captures illustrated highlight another aspect of carp fishing, the individual approach. Only one depicts the capture of a carp by the 'modern method'; the remainder portray what would currently be considered improvisation, which was, and always will be, an essential part of a successful carp-fishing approach.

Hugh Sheringham at Cheshunt

The quotation which starts this chapter is from Mr Shering-ham's account of the capture of this fish. He was not the most successful of the Cheshunt anglers, nor was his fish the biggest to come from the water, but I think his narrative is one of the earliest pieces of writing to convey the feel of carp fishing, to elevate it to a plane higher than just fishing.

Albert Buckley at Mapperley

We have BB to thank for the detailed account of Albert Buckley's astonishing catch of carp from Mapperley Reservoir. He went to the trouble of obtaining it for *The Fisherman's Bedside Book* and reproduced it again in *Confessions*. It is an exciting story and Mr Buckley's 26lb mirror was the biggest carp to be caught in this country until Redmire Pool was discovered.

Dick Walker at Redmire Pool

Sheringham and Buckley were both float anglers; the next carp of real significance also fell to float-fishing tactics. That fish was the first of the Redmire monsters, a carp of 31lb 4oz which was landed by Bob Richards in October 1951. This fish was stunningly eclipsed the following September by Richard Walker's massive common of 44lb. I read the tale of this capture with awe long before I became a carp fisher; the feat was acclaimed beyond the ranks of anglers and many feel that this extraordinary event was the initial trigger for the rapid expansion in the popularity of carp fishing.

13 September 1952: Dick Walker and Pete Thomas at Redmire Pool. '. . . he switched on the electric lamp. We saw a great expanse of golden flank as the fish rolled.'

Chris Yates at Redmire Pool

Perhaps surprisingly, Dick Walker's record survived for nearly thirty years, until 16 June 1980, when Chris Yates hooked and landed a stalked fish of 51lb 8oz – at Redmire Pool. Because of the circumstances of the claim this fish is not an official record, although it is the record in the eyes of the vast majority of carp men and on the record list of the National Association of Specialist Anglers. It is a measure of the acceptance of Chris Yates's fish in the carp world that no subsequent claim has been forthcoming for the capture of a record carp, although at least two other acceptable fish have been caught above the old record weight of 44lb. Will Chris's fish remain the king for as long as the Buckley and Walker fish did?

These landmark fish span a period of three-quarters of a century. Their capture has one thing in common: not one of the fish was caught by what is now regarded by many as *the* carp-fishing method. If there is a lesson to be learned from that it is not an immediately obvious one: at least two of the fish were caught as a result of the use of the carp-fishing method of the time! If the anglers concerned had had available to them the baits and presentations now current, and had wished to avail themselves of them (Yatesy for one feels that bare-hook rigs are unethical), then our carp-fishing history might read very differently. That is idle speculation. What has gone before *is* history and the pages that follow concentrate on the problems of modern carp fishing.

Ritchie Macdonald at Yateley

Ritchie's splendid Yateley mirror carp of 45lb 12oz is the biggest of numerous big fish to fall to the modern carp-fishing method. An increase in the number of carp anglers has, over the last fifteen years or so, led to an increasing competitiveness in the carp world. Out of this competition have emerged a number of great thinkers and innovators, including Rod Hutchinson, Fred Wilton, Lenny Middleton with Kevin Maddocks, and others less well known for their forward thinking. Out of their individual efforts new methods and baits have become available, and new standards by which success is measured have been set.

Purists would argue that carp fishing is no better for the progress that has been made, but those who are now able to enjoy the thrill of catching carp without having to wait half a

16 June 1980: Chris Yates at Redmire Pool.
'The line tightened immediately and I struck into something that ran
diagonally across the shallows . . .' Chris with his great mirror of
51lb 6oz.

October 1984: Ritchie Macdonald at Yateley North Lake.
'My feeling was of total achievement!' Ritchie with his magnificent
fish of 45lb 12oz.

lifetime for a bite would probably disagree. Carp catching is now a practical proposition for anyone who wishes to turn his mind to it. It is not easy, but it is easier. It can be hard work, but for most it is a labour of love and the more you put into it the greater your rewards will be. It is to be enjoyed – though carp fishing being the glorious frustration it undoubtedly is, there are times when we all forget that it is supposed to be a pleasure. Sometimes it isn't and we all suffer when we are fishing for carp that are beyond our ability and the indicators just won't move.

Catching carp is a thing of a moment, but the build-up to that moment can be painstaking, frustrating and time-consuming – which was undoubtedly true of some of the captures we have looked at here.

The main objective of fishing for carp is to catch carp. But, if your carp fishing is only about catching, you may suffer and lose interest. Carp fishing is the great escape and the catching of carp is just an occasional – though necessary – part of the addiction.

2

Glaphad – An Appraisal

One of the greatest difficulties in writing about carp fishing is the variety of the problems facing the readers. Waters differ, and the pressure on each water is impossible to assess. It is perhaps possible to put waters into categories, but even then the individual waters within the various categories fall into numerous subdivisions, and each water throws up its own problems. Coming to terms with the water you are fishing is largely a question of defining to yourself the major difficulty in catching carp from that water. Solving that *major* problem will carry you a long way towards catching the water's carp.

Here are two simple examples of waters at opposite ends of the scale. Given a big water with a handful of carp in it, the hardest nut to crack is likely to be fish location. On such a water

The waiting game . . . I'm not catching, so what's the problem? Your mind should be working like a computer before, during and after most of your carp sessions.

the fish may not have become tackle-conscious through repeated capture, so if you can find the fish you could be in with a chance of catching them. On the other hand, with the same number of carp in a pressured one-acre pool you are looking at a completely different set of problems. Location will not be difficult; you will have to concentrate your thinking on bait, bait application and presentation.

Those are two extreme examples and between the two lies a range of waters, all different. If you don't know how to go about solving the riddle of catching carp from your water, have a long hard think about it. List the main essentials which go towards making successful carp fishing and assess realistically the extent to which you have come to terms with each. Glaphad is a mnemonic, a memory aid. It stands for the following:

Going bait   You've got to have a bait that's good enough to enable you to catch the fish you're after.
Location   You must be fishing where there are fish.
Application   Are you getting the best out of your bait?
Presentation   Is your presentation good enough to let you hook the carp you are fishing for?
Hotspots   Fish location may not be good enough; you may have to pinpoint feeding location even further with difficult fish.
Ability   This doesn't imply that you have to be a natural carp angler; few of us are. It means that you will have to be able to meet the demands that fishing for carp may make on you.
Determination   If you've got enough of this you'll crack all the others.

Some of these areas are dealt with in greater detail elsewhere within the book, and glaphad pervades all the chapters that follow, but I'll briefly expand some of the points here. Carp fishing is a demanding pursuit and the more difficult the carp you are after the more demands it will make on you.

Going bait doesn't really need expanding at this stage. A bait which works on one water may not work, or can have already been fished out, on another. Your bait may be from a tackle dealer's fridge, or from a tin, or may be one of your own that you've been baiting up with for months. Whatever it is, the carp has got to take it in its mouth and give a strikable indication before you can put the landing net under it.

Location can be one of the hardest parts of carp fishing – or one of the easiest. On big waters it can be very frustrating, particularly in changing conditions when the fish are moving

Bob Davis whiling away the hours on a southern big fish water.

round a great deal. You can spend time fishing with no carp within hundreds of yards of you, and you may have to move frequently to stay in touch with the fish. Fishing big, understocked waters can be very rewarding, but it is often far from being a leisurely, peaceful pursuit. Moving once during a long session requires a degree of self-discipline; moving more than once demands a level of dedication few of us can lift ourselves to, whatever frustrations we are suffering and however great the potential prize.

Application of bait cannot be covered in a paragraph, and it can't be explained in a chapter. No two situations are ever exactly the same when it comes to applying bait to a swim, or to a water. To a water? Yes, because application of bait doesn't just mean on the day, or during a session. It also applies to the establishing of a bait over a period of weeks, or months.

Presentation of bait to some extent overlaps with application, but regard application as the use of free offerings, whether for prebaiting or for groundbaiting, and presentation as the use of the hookbait. Application is a decisive factor in determining presentation, though. On one occasion when I was going through a crisis of confidence over the presentation I was using on Darenth Tip Lake, that experienced carp man, the wise Dennis Davies, reassured me with the words: 'Once they've got confidence in the bait they will take it on almost any

A familiar sight: dawn with the mist drifting off the water and the indicators poised – or Superglued? That morning they were merely poised and I caught two good fish.

Opportunist fish. I heard it leap in the early hours almost seventy yards from the baits. I reeled in, tied a fresh PVA stringer, cast towards the sound the fish had made – and was away within minutes. The fish weighed 19lb 10oz.

presentation.' They are words I often remind myself of.

Hotspots are discussed in greater detail at a later stage.

Ability is something you must have in some measure on all waters, in far greater measure on others. On some waters you will have to be able to cast a long way; on others you will need to be a good stalker; on others you will have to be able to wait long periods without the indicators moving. The more angling ability you have, in the natural sense, the easier you will find it to make your own assessments and come to terms with the special requirements of each water. One of the great beauties of carp fishing is that you don't have to be a natural angler to be successful at catching carp. But the less natural ability you have the greater will be your need for that greatest of all carp-fishing assets – the final element of glaphad.

Determination is described in his exceptional book *Still-Water Angling* by the late Dick Walker in the following wise words, among many others, on the approach to big-fish angling:

Besides confidence, there is another element in your approach to big fish catching which is not always there to begin with, but which I believe anyone can cultivate. It is a mixture of enthusiasm, determination and persistence . . . That must be your attitude. If you think that no fish can matter that much,

*'It must matter tremendously that you catch the fish you are after.'
Dick Walker's words from the early 1950s, which is the date of this fine Redmire study. Kevin Clifford kindly provided this previously unpublished picture of Dick.*

you will fail. It must matter tremendously that you should catch the fish you are after.

I could quote at great length from *Still-Water Angling*. Some of the technical material seems dated, obviously, but the more general writing is timeless, perceptive, clear-headed common sense and well worth reading and re-reading.

Carp anglers are looked upon as a patient breed. Some may be, but many of us are not and I certainly don't consider myself to be a patient carp angler. The waiting involved between fish on waters where the fishing is slow I tend to find irksome – although on occasions it can seem the most pleasant way of life. But for the most part I do find waiting hard work, and I will close this chapter with Dick Walker's words of nearly forty years ago on the subject:

When you have done your best in every way you can think of, you must wait . . . Waiting is, indeed, hard work. Catching big fish involves a great deal of hard work, of which waiting is only a part. Perhaps that is why you feel so tremendous a sense of satisfaction when you succeed.

3

First Carp
by Vic Cranfield

When did you first realise that you wanted to be a carp fisher? For me it happened late, but luckily not too late. I started fishing when I was about eleven and stopped when I was about fourteen, when I started to see girls as more than a nuisance. To cut a long story short, I didn't start fishing again until I was thirty-two years old, and married with two children – and that was by accident.

I had recently moved house and was in the garden when I noticed my next door neighbour checking his tackle in preparation for the new season. One word led to another and before I knew it I had arranged to accompany my neighbour on his first trip of the season.

That was it! One trip and I was hooked again, and as time went by I started to concentrate more and more on the better-quality fish. It was about this time that I started to read everything I could lay my hands on to do with fishing. Inevitably I got hold of a copy of Jack Hilton's book *Quest for Carp*. Now, if you have been lucky enough to read this book you will understand me when I say that I was absolutely overwhelmed by it. If I read that book once I read it half a dozen times! I couldn't put it down. To me it was everything that carp fishing is about – the carp fisher's bible, you might say.

Well, that was it, a carp fisher I would be. That brought me to the first of many problems that were to dog me on the way to my first carp: where do I go, or whom do I speak to to help me get started? I didn't know one carp angler in those days, or know of any carp clubs or organisations. So it was back to the good old library to pore over the weekly and monthly angling publications to get all the information I could.

My first carp rod was a Jack Hilton (it had to be, didn't it?) from Alan Brown's. It was an 11-foot compound-taper rod of 1½lb test curve and I built it myself. I already had a Mitchell 300 which I loaded with 8lb BS Maxima line. Initially my end tackle was no. 2 Jack Hilton hook on a hooklength of about 12 inches tied to a Berkley swivel and fished with a running 1oz Arlesey bomb. All I had to do now was find a water that contained carp. I found that more by luck than by judgement. Fourways Fisheries had an advertisement in *Angling Times* for a lake at Potters Bar in Hertfordshire. It was a syndicate water and limited to forty members. I couldn't believe my good fortune.

I phoned Fourways Fisheries and asked if I could go and have a look at the lake before I parted with my money. After missing the turning a couple of times I found the track that led down to the water. I parked my car in the small car park and climbed the embankment to the lake's edge; I couldn't believe what I was looking at! The lake was about 1¼ acres of sheer paradise. I suppose you would call the bank I was standing on the dam wall. It was about sixty yards long and fairly straight. It had lilies along virtually all its length reaching out four or five yards from the bank. The other banks converged until they met at the far end of the lake about 150 yards away. That was the shallow end, and it was covered in reeds.

The two long banks were lined with overhanging shrubs and trees which trailed their branches into the water. It was early June, the time was about 6 pm, the sun was shining, and there was the odd dark shape cruising about beneath the surface. If that doesn't sell the lake to you I'm sure I don't know what will. My cheque was in the post that night.

I started fishing the lake on Tuesday nights at first because of work commitments. I've already described my end tackle. The bait was luncheon meat fished straight on the hook. I didn't know about the hair; in fact, as you have no doubt gathered, I didn't know a great deal about anything as regards carp fishing then. But what I lacked in knowledge I made up for in enthusiasm.

My first trip to the lake was a make-do-and-mend kind of a session. I only had one carp rod so I took another rod along and put this out for tench. This was just an ordinary 11-foot general coarse-fishing rod. The carp rod was baited with luncheon meat and put out to my right, close to some overhanging trees. A few free samples were thrown in around the hookbait. The tench rod I baited with good old sweetcorn, lobbed it out in front of me, next to some lilies, then threw in some orange-sized balls of mashed bread and bran. I set up my garden chair and waited for it to happen. Oh yes, I nearly forgot. I had also purchased a pair of Optonics the previous Saturday so I was a real specimen hunter by this time!

I had my son Scott with me and had just sorted out the sleeping arrangements when the left-hand Optonic burst into life. The tench put up one hell of a fight, then got snagged up, which meant me going in for it. It was worth it, though, because it weighed in at 4lb 15oz and was in pristine condition. That was it for that trip. I had the dolly on the carp rod twitch 4 inches up the needle, but that was all and I left for work at just after 6 am.

After that I had another carp rod sent down from Alan Brown's. This was the same as the original rod but in black, as against the honey colour, and was already built. I now had two carp rods and was a real carp fisher!

The next trip was the Tuesday following the tench capture. I fished another swim, this one down the left-hand side of the lake. The spot was to become a favourite of mine and I fished it until I caught a carp. The swim had a large tree to the right of it which dangled its branches into the lake about twenty feet out, but directly in front. That's where the right-hand bait went – as close to the branches as possible. The left-hand bait went under an overhanging shrub to the left of the swim. By poking around under the shrub I found that there was nothing in the water to snag the line – if I was lucky enough to get a take. I was able to poke the rod right under the shrub, release the line to drop the bait into position, leave the bail arm open and put the rod back on its rest. I was fishing this bait at right angles to the rod and using luncheon meat on both rods. The trip was uneventful except for the odd twitch and two- or three-inch lift.

The following session was different – I actually had a take! This came to the rod fishing by the trailing branches but within minutes the hook pulled out. Keep going! On the next trip something happened that I had only previously read about.

Everything was set up. It was about 9.30 p.m. and I was thinking of turning in when off went the right-hand Optonic. I leant into the fish and it felt good. Within minutes I had it close to the bank and the bent rod was steadily bouncing up and down to the lunges of the fish. Suddenly everything went solid; there was no movement through the rod; the water went completely calm. I thought to myself that there was no weed there that it could be snagged in, so what could it be?

I tried heaving on the rod, then suddenly releasing the tension, putting the rod back in the rests and waiting – but to no avail. All that was left was to pull for a break. I was reluctant to go in as I couldn't feel the fish any more, so I picked the rod up again and slowly heaved. Nothing, so I heaved a bit more. Could I feel something moving? More pressure. Yes! Some-

Vic with one of the many fish he has caught since that first magical capture.

thing *was* moving and very slowly it surfaced, looking huge in the fading light. Yes, it was definitely the biggest I'd had – the biggest branch, that is. I had only read about fish transferring hooks but now it had happened. One minute you have a fish lunging on the end of your line, the next moment you're banking a great branch. Two fish lost in as many weeks – I was *gutted*. The next couple of trips were just as frustrating inasmuch as I was having runs but they were stopping at various stages without developing properly. Sometimes the dolly would stop at the top of the needle, or half-way up, then three-quarters of the way. I didn't know what to do. In fact I was so choked I almost didn't go the following week, but I decided to go and try something different.

We arrived at the lake at about 6.30 p.m. – my daughter and I. Paula had been wanting to go fishing with me for ages but my wife, adopting the typical protective role, had always said no. This time she had relented and there we were. We set up in the swim that I had been fishing on previous Tuesday nights. As we arrived a lad was returning a carp he had just caught. Neither Paula nor I had seen a big carp on the bank before so we went round to have a look. It seemed huge and weighed about 17½ lb, filling me with confidence.

The new method I was going to employ was freelining. I'd decided that the half-hearted runs I had been having may have resulted from the carp being able to feel the drag of the dolly as it was pulled up the needle. The thing to do was scrap the dolly, and that's what I did. Bail arm open, no dolly, no lead; indication would be the line being pulled through the Optonic.

Again the baits were put in the same places – the right-hand rod out in front under the overhanging branches and the left-hand bait under the bush on my left. Again the bait was luncheon meat. All we had to do was wait – now where have I heard that before? We turned in about 10.30 p.m. The last thing I remember was looking at the Optonics trying to will them into life.

It was one second after I closed my eyes (or so it seemed at the time; actually it was four hours) that the left-hand Optonic burst into life. My heart leapt into my mouth, the bed-chair almost collapsing under me in my frantic haste to get to the rod. This was no three- or four-inch lift; this was the Optonic in full song, and it wasn't going to stop. I stumbled to the rod. As I closed the bail arm and lifted the rod it was pulled severely to the left and almost wrenched from my grasp. The fish had taken the bait from under the bush and was taking advantage of the fact that I was half asleep by ploughing up the margin to my left. I was waking up fast and applying sidestrain with the rod top level with the water. The fish started to swing out into the middle of the lake, much to my relief. It was at this point that Paula joined her shaking dad at the water's edge and asked if she could help, bless her. I asked her to dip my other rod and put the landing net in the water ready. I was shaking so much it was a wonder she could understand me.

By this time the fish was tiring and I was slowly bringing it nearer to the waiting net. This is where the fun starts. This was my first carp, and also the first fish of this size that it had been my good fortune to hook. It was also going to be Paula's first attempt at netting *any* fish, let alone one of this size. Although I had never caught a carp before I knew that this was no tiddler. And just to make me feel a bit more confident the only net I had was a 30-inch one, which was going to be wielded by a novice for a novice. Hallelujah!

To her eternal credit Paula netted the carp at her fifth attempt, and that was only after calmly walking away and returning with my torch so she could 'see what I'm doing, Dad'! The fish finally went into the net; I bit the line and with Paula's help picked up the net and fish and staggered up the bank on the verge of a physical and nervous breakdown.

As we uncovered the fish from the folds of the net the thrill of elation that ran through me was beyond description, and similar feelings were going through my daughter as well, I think. In the light of the torch the fish looked huge and Paula asked if it was as big as the one we had seen earlier. I said that it looked similar but had a feeling that it was bigger. When we weighed it the scales showed 21lb 1oz and after deducting the sling we were left with a mighty 20lb 8oz. My first carp! I couldn't believe it and wondered if I was still asleep. I looked at Paula and she looked at me, the silly grin on her face mirroring the one on mine. To look at us it would have been hard to say who had caught the fish – but I suppose that in those circumstances we both had. It was *our* first carp.

4

Hooking Carp

Hooking carp falls into one of two basic categories, and the angler has to have a clear idea which method he is using before casting out. An angler can either fish with diligence and strike the hook into the carp, or he can fish a variation of the modern carp-fishing method and wait for the fish to hook itself.

All bare-hook rigs are bolt rigs designed to make the fish partially hook itself. They do not always succeed in their design but that is the clear intention behind their use. Each part of a modern set-up is an integral piece of the whole design. Heavy leads direct on the line are there to set the point of the hook; run clips, back-stops or foam are there to help pull the hook in further, and to keep the pressure on the point; monkey climbers and heavy indicators also help increase the resistance against which the partially hooked fish is pulling. Needle-sharp hooks, chemically sharpened carbon-steel hooks, fixed leads, back-stops, heavy indicators – all are part of the self-hooking principle and if you are fishing to make the carp run you must keep looking to your tackle to make sure you are getting the best out of what you are doing. The bare-hook presentation is a method rather than a rig, and angling considerations must be applied to its use just as much as to float fishing, paternostering and swimfeeder fishing.

Don't confuse bare-hook bolt fishing with the more sensitive forms of angling, in which you set the hook by striking at bite indications fished for in an angling situation. Nowadays *angling* methods tend to be applied to carp fishing only when they have to be, as in the situation described in Chapter 8, or in Brian Skoyles's floater fishing. In most other situations the modern carp-fishing method prevails, whether it is still producing results or not. But on many waters carp are now so accustomed to being on their guard against hooking themselves on suspect boiled baits, and particles, that it could be that their defences are well and truly down when it comes to the use of methods which depend on the *elimination* of resistance, as opposed to the application of it.

Bill Walford with a lovely example of a linear mirror carp.

A method's effectiveness on any given water will bear a direct relationship to the use of the method on that water over the previous months and years. In other words, carp learn by their mistakes and if you are not catching, or your catch rate is slower than you feel it should be, it is possible that you are using a method that has lost its effectiveness because of its past success on your water. It is up to the angler to assess realistically the actual effectiveness of what he is doing.

Try to get inside the carp's mind and understand what you need to do to produce a strikable indication. Carp can only 'think' within the framework of their most recent experiences, so you must think outside that framework to try to outwit them. On most carp waters the carp *are* eating baits, so stationary indicators do not mean that they 'aren't having it' – they mean that the fish have wised up to the predictability of your presentation.

If you are *fishing* for carp rather than trying to make them bolt, then you must think your way through the new set of circumstances. Shut your mind to the modern carp-fishing method and go back to what used to be basics. Freelining, fixed paternostering, or link-leger set-ups could well confuse the carp on some waters and any of these set-ups used in conjunction with paste baits or lightly skinned baits could, if the angler is prepared to strike at comparatively small lifts of the indicator, bring dividends. In situations where you are trying to minimise resistance and strike at bite indications rather than runs, don't fish monkey climbers. The old favourites – silver-paper cylinders, rings made of plastic aquarium tubing, or washing-up liquid bottle tops – will be more suitable.

The more you understand about presentation the easier you will find it to apply your own thinking to the changing situation on the water or waters you are fishing. There is no

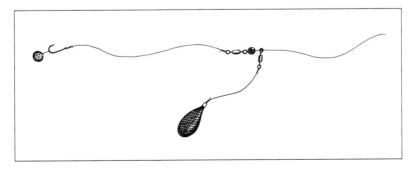

Link leger for sensitive bite indication.

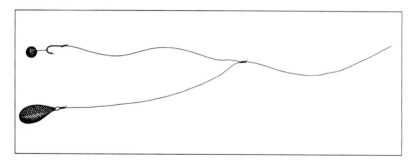

Fixed paternoster – even more sensitive.

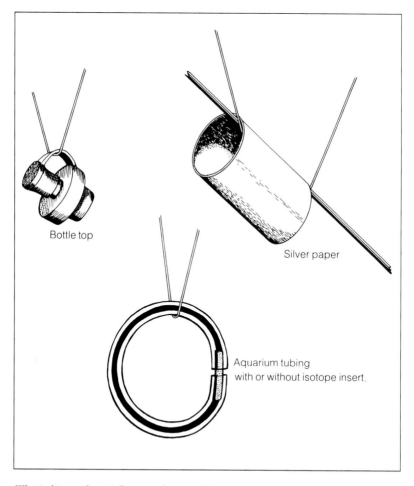

Bottle top

Silver paper

Aquarium tubing
with or without isotope insert.

*The indicator doesn't have to be a monkey climber! I've spent many
weeks staring at these three options which are very useful where
resistance is more of a hindrance than a help.*

The splendid lines of a near 20lb common carp.

such thing as an old-fashioned presentation. All the tackle arrangements described in this book have caught their fair share of carp, but over the last few years trickery has replaced angling on many waters and thinking has become very stereotyped.

You have to start somewhere on presentation; we all do. Go to your water with a fairly clear idea of how you want to fish but be ready to accept that you have got it wrong and that you may have to change your method, or at least modify it. It doesn't matter how long you've been carp fishing; have confidence in the fact that your thinking is just as valid as anyone else's. Most people are catching carp on other people's ideas, but the more successful carp anglers can think on their feet and make changes to outwit the carp while they are fishing. Adapt whatever is available to your own thinking and understanding; that way you will find it is easier to adjust what you are doing to suit the prevailing conditions and the unpredictability of the carp *you* are fishing for.

The first time you think something out for yourself, or in consultation with a friend, and that thinking catches carp, you will have made a big step forward in your carp fishing.

5

I Got You Babe!

Rightly or wrongly, we all like to pose with our carp. Those who are critical of the practice dismiss it as an act of egoism. I don't think it is. I feel that it's the commemoration of a moment of personal triumph. After all, we get photographed on our wedding day and most of us love carp far more than . . .

Hooking carp is a means to an end. It isn't really possible to treat them humanely while you are playing and landing them, although an element of respect for them can be reflected in your whole approach to carp fishing. If you are on a water that is beyond your capabilities, go and fish elsewhere. Don't resort to extremes which could damage or kill the fish.

You will see ultra-light hooklengths recommended for carp fishing. These usually seem to be recommended by suppliers of bait – presumably because plenty of indicator action will sell more of the bait in use. Leaving hooks in carp is bad enough; playing them to the point of total exhaustion on an inadequate hooklink *can kill them*. Use a hooklink of a breaking strain which will give you a chance of landing the fish within a

Successful carp man Russ Rodgers bringing a Cuttle Mill fish to the net.

*Easy baby! Dennis Johncock nets a fish for the author at a Society
Llandrindod Wells fish-in.*

reasonable period of time. Some hard-fighting carp can take
upwards of fifteen minutes to subdue on standard tackle; to risk
having to play fish for periods of longer than an hour is
completely irresponsible.

I once found a pectoral fin in swim 1 at Waveney valley – on
the bank! The boat boys had been on the water the week before
chucking their end tackles into inaccessible places in the
marginal snags. Such tactics are equivalent to an admission that
the carp in the water are beyond your capabilities; there is no
shame in encountering carp you can't catch. Go elsewhere and
get it right, then go back and try again – fairly.

Believe it or not, there is a (very minor) school of thought
which claims – totally irresponsibly – that you are in order if
you leave your baits out fishing for you while you leave the
water. If you encounter the practice don't bring shame on
yourself and carp fishing by lowering yourself to that level.

When you do get a fish on the bank treat it like a baby. If you
are photographing it right away, spread sacks and a groundsheet and let the carp lie in the landing-net mesh in the water's
edge until the camera gear is ready. If you are allowed to sack

A Cuttle Mill 19lb plus. Note the canvas cradle. There is at least one of these in each swim at Cuttle. We could do with one of the tackle dealer innovators to come up with a portable version because they really are ideal for unhooking fish.

*Chris Shelley from Stoke's Rod and Line coping with the problems
of photography on a hard bank. Note the groundsheet, sacks and
water container; the fish is being held low to the ground as an extra
precaution.*

the fish do so, using a large sack of soft material that allows a
good flow of water through it.

If you have to retain the fish over a period of hours while
awaiting suitable light for photography, give careful thought to
the positioning of the sack. Find a margin with some depth and
use a long extension cord so that the fish can move around and
select the most comfortable level in the water. Keep checking
the sack to make sure that the fish is upright and breathing, and
never be tempted to bring the fish out to show people until you
are going to take the pictures.

Prepare the area for the photo session before taking the sack
out of the water. Lay out a groundsheet and sacks if the bank is
hard and keep a container of water handy for repeated wettings
of the fish. If the carp has been sacked for some time be
prepared to cope with its liveliness when you are trying to
handle it. Get as many friends as possible to assist. You can't
rush photographing carp properly and they are well capable of

Back she goes, handled with care. Hold the fish until you are sure it is all right and capable of staying upright, then let it go.

surviving a period out of the water without suffering permanent damage, but when they are on the bank they are out of their natural environment and must be treated with affection and care.

Try to avoid brace or multiple shots. There is a strong temptation to 'double up' when you have had more than one fish, but most carp anglers have had good fish in quick succession and photographed them individually. I've had two twenties within a couple of hours three times, but I've no brace shots of them. I've got a number of multiple shots going back to my early carping days, but attitudes have changed with the growth of carp fishing and there is an increasing awareness of the need to care for the carp at all times.

Show the fish the respect they are entitled to from the moment you tackle up and cast out to the moment you put them back to fight another day. We all love to catch immaculate carp. When you are fortunate enough to land one, try to make sure it stays that way for the next lucky captor.

6

The Carp-Fishing Method

In 1981 Greg Fletcher and I were made aware of the method of carp fishing that had been accounting for a great many fish in the south of England – the hair. Some time later the method was publicised through the writings of Lenny Middleton in *Coarse Angler* and Kevin Maddocks in his book *Carp Fever*. Carp catching was suddenly made to sound very easy: semolina-based baits laced with 5 millilitres of flavour; rock-hard baits tied to the hook; increase resistance with a tightly clipped up line; sit back and await screaming runs. It sounded good. We decided to give it a whirl – as you would!

Being aware of a method is one thing; it is quite another coming to terms with it and using it to your best advantage in a carp-fishing situation. It is far easier to *think* catching carp than it is to turn the dreaming into reality. This is a mental barrier

Thinker and innovator Lenny Middleton with just one of the many fish he caught on his invention – the hair rig.

43

We did catch before the bare hook rigs became popular. Here that fine carp angling writer Jim Gibbinson is pictured with one of ten Bysing Wood doubles caught in one afternoon!

we all have to face head on and conquer. You must have the confidence to make what you are doing work. We quickly found that there were practical problems to come to terms with if we wanted to get the best out of the method. (It's amazing how much the application of the basic bare-hook presentation has changed over a six-year period.)

Initially Greg and I didn't catch fish on the bare-hook rigs. I didn't have enough confidence in the bait changes needed and

A good water to come to terms with carp fishing on; Lymm Dam in Cheshire.

Fletch was a bit dubious of the presentation itself. Our pooling of ideas and exchanging of notes helped us come to terms with what we were trying to do and we gradually formed a clear picture of what was happening – why we were, or weren't catching – and we were able to make adjustments and improvise as we went along.

Concentrating on a method of catching carp over a reasonable period of time teaches you a great deal about a number of aspects of carp fishing, so there were spin-offs from our struggles with the bare-hook presentations. Solving one problem leads to new difficulties and even the use of a simple method becomes an evolutionary process.

Much of our early hair fishing was at Roman Lakes, and was long-range work. We had to cast long distances to reach the fish, learn to bait up at range, learn to cope with tangles and, most important of all, learn to assess the ups and downs of our successes and failures.

It is hard to be realistic in assessing progress. You have to have some idea of the water's day-to-day potential and measure your results against what you feel the water is capable of producing for you in the prevailing conditions. If you want to go on to fish the difficult waters you must learn to catch consistently from hungry waters like Roman Lakes. Don't accept no for an answer on a water where a blank day means you are getting it wrong.

Throughout that period at Roman, Greg and I used long-range rods, but not rods designed for extreme range. What is the difference? Long-range rods will fish effectively up to 120 yards or so; extreme-range rods will enable you to fish further out than that. I was using Alan Brown Spiraflex LRIs, compound-taper 12-footers of 2lb test curve. Greg's rods were Sportex 11-footers of 2¼lb test curve (the original Kevin Maddocks blank, I think). The initial set-up consisted of 6lb BS Maxima reel line, 11lb BS Sylcast shock leaders to withstand the force of the long-range casting, 2–2½oz leads fished direct on the line (with or without a back-stop), protective bead, stop swivel, 6lb BS mono hooklength, ½–2-inch fine line hair tied on the bend of the hook, line clipped up tight. The presentation, and each modification we used, is illustrated. Initially indication was by means of a plastic indicator on a vertical needle. Tactics were fairly standard for a water that responded well to hard boiled baits and bare-hook presentations.

After a slowish start we caught a great many fish from the water, as did a number of other people. Baits were really very simple to start with – the better the smell the more fish you caught, provided you could cast to the fish, and on some days this was easier than on others. Every indication was of a belting run – for a while – but the fish did start to wise up surprisingly quickly. Results slowed, twitches occurred – the line whacking out of the clip and the run stopping before it had really started. The fish were still on the baits but soon learned to avoid the one

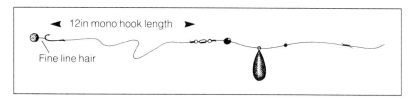

Initial set-up.

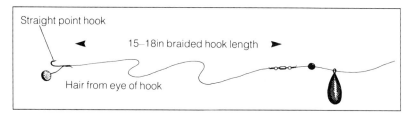

First change.

Roman Lakes where Greg and I worked at coming to terms with the bare hook presentations and boiled baits.

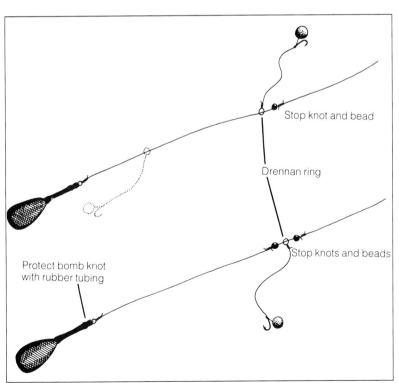

Stop knot and bead

Drennan ring

Stop knots and beads

Protect bomb knot with rubber tubing

The bomb on the end of the line aids long casting. The set-up allows very short bolt rigs to be fished on silt bottoms.

47

tied to the hook. We were fishing 9–12-inch hooklengths and shortening or lengthening the hooklength revived results. The carp were able to avoid being caught on a predictable presentation but any sort of change seemed to throw them.

We were consistently fishing at ranges of 90–110 yards and this in itself threw up some tactical problems. Baiting up at 100 yards plus is a problem, although casting that distance is within the capabilities of most with a good carbon long-range rod. At the time the most commonly used boilie catapult was the Black Widow, which tears your hands to pieces and won't catapult a boiled bait 100 yards. I couldn't get on with the Black Widow at all and soon became the proud owner of a Barnett Diablo, which doesn't tear your hands to pieces, will catapult a boiled bait of the right size over 100 yards, and is far more accurate than the Black Widow. It costs more, a few quid more. Carbon costs a great deal more than glass but I never see anyone fishing at range with glass rods nowadays. On a number of waters I've watched anglers firing out loose feed to sixty or seventy yards, then casting their hookbaits over a hundred yards. I'm not suggesting that it's absolutely vital to have loose feed round the hookbait, but much of the time I prefer to, and it certainly doesn't make sense to draw the fish away from the hookbait through the inaccurate application of groundbait.

As results became increasingly hit-and-miss on the basic hair presentation, we started trying a variety of hooks, hooklength materials, length of hooklength, position of the hair, length of the hair, bait on the bottom or off it, foaming the butt ring, bomb on the end of the line, and any other variation of a theme

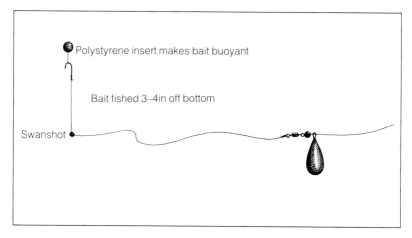

Polystyrene insert makes bait buoyant

Bait fished 3–4in off bottom

Swanshot

We now balance the bait exactly, but that didn't occur to us then.

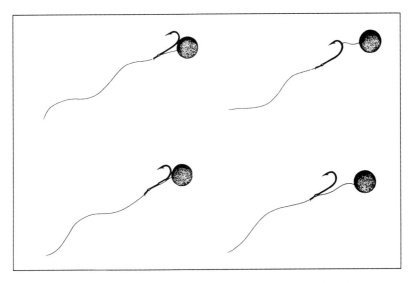

The way in which the bait is mounted on the hook can make a lot of difference in some situations. Give your presentation a great deal of thought.

Fletch easing a lively Roman Lakes double towards the net.

Gently does it! The rod is held high to give as much cushion as possible against any last-minute surge, and the fish is led over the net.

which seemed worth trying. It soon became clear that the modern method was a subtle form of presentation, not the all-conquering answer to a carp man's prayer.

We only ever fished two swims on the water; that way we became familiar with the hotspots. They can be very localised and even casting a hundred yards into an apparently featureless expanse of open water can be a very precise matter. It took us a long time to stumble on one or two of the hotspots, and even then we could never be sure that the bait was in exactly the right place. It was a question of casting at a far-bank feature and sensing when the range was right.

Roman Lakes has a very silty bottom, so the lessons we learned there can't be applied to all waters. The 'bomb on the end of the line' presentation worked well there; it is a presentation that is ideal for fishing bolt rigs over silt and isn't as effective on hard bottoms. Changes of flavour worked well, because Roman is a hungry water and these were the early days of the bare-hook rigs. I don't like to look on any carp as guinea-pigs, I love fishing for all of them, but waters like Roman Lakes can teach you a lot. You are either getting it right or getting it wrong and there is very little in between. Stick with the busy, hungry waters with a fair head of carp in them to start with and assess your results realistically (without being competitive about it) against what the other anglers on the water are doing. It is a good way to learn, or re-learn, your carp fishing. I go back to Roman Lakes from time to time because I like the place and the carp there are good teachers.

The modern carp-fishing method is a basis. The carp wise up to it and their natural instincts help them build up a resistance to it. The slightest modification can confuse them, so always be ready to adapt what you are doing on the evidence that your indicators give you.

7

Carp Setting
by Dave Preston

You may wonder about the title of this chapter. It does in fact mean something to me – about the way I, and probably many other carp anglers, go about fishing. 'Carp setting' is derived from goal setting, a technique used by the richest men in the world, the best athletes and the top sportsmen. It simply means thinking about just what it is you want to achieve, thinking about it so much that it drives you on until you get it.

Because carp angling appeals to those who want the bigger fish, goal setting is part of the programme of most carp anglers, although it does pay to temper down the brash forcefulness implied by goal setting and bide one's time. The story that follows illustrates this.

There are several pools containing the odd big carp that I have returned to on and off over a fair few years, any one of which could have completely absorbed my time and energy for a few seasons until I'd caught the carp I was after. Leach Pit was one of them. It contained two carp over 20lb, until one of them died; all the other were 14lb or less, and most weighed less than 8lb.

Each time I returned to the water I'd think that the problems that had previously seemed insurmountable would shrink into insignificance before my most recently found skills. Sometimes they did, but the new skills often failed to provide the answers I needed to catch *that* fish, so after a few blanks, or a few tiddler commons, I'd move on elsewhere, wondering what I needed to do, needed to know, to get the big one.

First catfood baits, then sweetcorn, then bolt rigs, then the hair rig and boilies. The hair rig had to work, didn't it? The fish were accustomed to the super-fine lines of the match anglers who frequented the pool. It didn't do the trick!

When a rig I tried worked on another pool I thought I'd cracked it. A 3oz bomb locked on to 11lb monofil, 14-inch hooklength, size 6 Lion d'Or with bait cube tied on the bend of the hook; rods at 45 degrees to the line and clipped up so tight that the spring of the rod would send the bomb flying at the slightest touch. The bait being tied tight to the bend meant the hook had to be in the fish's mouth; the 14-inch hooklength meant there was room for the fish to gain momentum and jar against the bomb – those carp were snatching at baits.

Not even this set-up was good enough for the Leach Pit carp. The rod tip would wobble before swinging back and – nothing. Occasionally a small common would get caught. Not good enough. It had to be a bait presentation problem. What I needed was an instantly attractive particle bait, which, I reasoned, had to be a particle boilie.

Fed up with rolling tiny little balls for boiling, I resolved to boil one mix of paste in one big ball in a plastic bag. It never works out quite as easily as you first think and the first mix 'melted' and ran out of the bag – which disintegrated. At the next attempt the bait remained solid enough for it to set and the plastic bag (a Woolworths freezer bag) didn't melt. Unfortunately that mix floated. Eventually the right mix was found, the correct boiling time (approximately one hour) worked out and Leach Pit was approached again.

On this particular day I paused at the bridge at one end of the pit. At this point the water shallows to a couple of inches, with house bricks, pram wheels and the like breaking surface here and there. Some small movement down below caught my eye. A ripple moved against the rest. Peering intently, I made out a dark shape gliding around in eighteen inches of water. A little later, two shapes – two small commons. Leaving the tackle I brushed through the overhanging bushes below to get right to the water's edge. Crouching, I could see the carp more clearly, coming into the bay in twos and threes, gliding about for a moment or two before leaving again.

Within a couple of minutes I was gone and back again with the bait ball and a knife. Hurriedly the ball was halved. One cut face was criss-crossed with knife cuts to make little (¹⁄₆ inch) squares, then a thin slice was cut off the half-ball to produce tiny cubes. Using a catapult to scatter the particles without moving the fish-scaring throwing arm, I noticed that the carp were hardly disturbed at all.

Fascinated, I watched three carp go down into the bottom in random spots, hardly pausing before they did so. Little puffs of silt mushroomed up here and there. They had quickly found the baited area and repeatedly sucked in the bottom, still hardly pausing after gliding around in tight circles. Within a couple of minutes they had slowed down and disappeared inside a

Dave with a brace of big doubles caught in quick succession while fishing over a bed of hemp.

veil of brown, silty water; little pieces of debris and fragments of weeds gushed to the surface amidst pea-sized bubbles. Then they were gone, only a few minutes after the bait had gone in. Quickly another handful of bait went in. I waited, uncomfortable with expectation. Two carp were there, milling around inside the silt, tails and backs easing out of the water. Too quickly they were gone again.

This time I put in twice as much bait before scrambling up the bank for the tackle. Before I had set up another two carp had been and gone. Making sure that there were no carp to scare, I cast out. I was feverish with haste, dreading that thump-thump-thump-thump-bump 'Any good?' of the notorious well-meaning pleasure angler. Bloosh, the bomb was out, shortly followed by the other and another handful of tiny bits of bait. Immediately four carp came in and went straight down into the baited area. Twitch after twitch but no runs, no bites for sure! I struck at two – but nothing. The carp didn't scare, they were so engrossed, but all too soon they were gone anyway.

Confused, I tried again with some more bait, and again. Each time the result was the same – carp in, twitches, bait gone, carp gone. Light dawned. They were feeding on tiny baits, not the ½-inch hookbait. Again the bait went in, and with it a handful of ½-inch cubes. Within minutes four commons re-entered the area, dashing about – and one big fat mirror. Ponderously it

Dave relaxing in the author's swim during a two-day session.

moved in, hardly twitching a fin, gliding under its own weight a couple of yards behind the commons. Just as it began to disappear inside the murky area the rod top wobbled violently. I struck before even the clip had released the line. A tremendous splashing and spraying of water, five separate bow waves, a slack line, a shocked, then disappointed angler.

Half-heartedly I rebaited. I knew they would not be back. I knew for sure that the one I wanted would not be back, but it was as easy to carry on as pack up. I cast out. Five minutes later the silt had resettled and the floating bits had drifted away. I lay back and was chewing over my rotten luck. Quite suddenly I saw three commons appear, followed slowly by the big one. I couldn't believe it. I froze and held my breath. Every movement of the fish could be seen. A few puffs of silt and the rod twitched. A great cloud of silt erupted as they tore off and away into the pool proper. No take. It had all happened before I could sit up. There was nothing I could do. I lay there just thinking when a big, fat shape wandered in. It was the big one again. I could hardly believe it. It puffed once at the bottom and jerked its head sideways and the buzzer screamed. I was in!

The rod hooped over, the water erupted. Line had to be given right away. As it gained speed I felt – I knew – that I must not give any more line. Clamping down, I splashed along the water's edge towards the open pool so as to pull on the fish from one side of it. It worked and it came around to its right, close in to the edge. I stepped back and swung the rod over to my left, and the carp carried on in its circle back towards the bay. As it entered the shallows it panicked and headed out and away, silt and water flying, its back out and thrashing.

It's difficult to turn these mad dashes directly away from you once they get more than a few yards of line. I let it tire itself on a good run. As it slowed I eased the pressure to keep it exerting itself. Thirty, forty, fifty yards it went. The carp was now reaching the danger point – any further and it could kite into the weeds on the left bank. I clamped up on the reel and the carp slowed to a stop and just wallowed. Winding in furiously, I ran along the bank to exert a direct side pull and began pumping it in. It was tired and apart from a few head jerks as I lowered the rod it came in easily, if slowly. When it was ten yards out I began walking back along the bank, maintaining smooth, steady pressure so as not to cause alarm. Like a dog, it followed behind.

A few moments and we were back to the net. The change in pull woke it up and, having regained its breath, it started on a run. I stopped it immediately, before it could really gain momentum, pulling from one side or the other every time it gained a direct pull on me. Five minutes later I pulled it round in a circle and netted it as it glided by in front. A second later it was on the bank, still fighting mad in the net.

It was a fine, fine mirror of 23½lb. Not the biggest ever, but the fish I was after.

8

The Channel

The modern carp-fishing method is effective, but bare-hook rigs and heavy bombs are designed to make the fish run. It is worth remembering that it isn't always wise to make them run, particularly when you are fishing near or against heavy snags.

We used to be far more inventive about our carp fishing before the rigs became available. In the 1970s and at the beginning of the 1980s I caught a great many carp by actually fishing for them – float fishing, light link-leger fishing, twitcher hitting on link legers and fixed paternosters. I think that some of the current carp anglers are perhaps growing up with the impression that you can catch a carp only by making it run, but that is far from being the case. It must be said that spooking the carp into screaming runs is the most practical form of fishing long sessions, but many anglers fish day, evening and morning sessions. At these times we could perhaps get far better results by *fishing* for carp rather than indulging in modern run-spooking trickery for the sake of it.

'Twitcher hitting' describes the form of carp fishing which involves striking on indications other than full runs. I learned the art through reading articles by Jim Gibbinson, and on a number of waters the method stood me in good stead. On other waters the carp steadfastly refused to give hittable indications other than rod-shaking runs, so the tactics aren't always valid.

By creating the right feeding situation it is sometimes possible to dictate the type of indication the carp will produce, give or take a twitch or two, and the water on which I was best able to produce the indications I wanted was Harlesthorpe Dam at Clowne. I should explain that an experience I had early in my fishing at the water convinced me that there was a big fish there and I put a great deal of thought and effort into bringing about its downfall.

My first encounter with the unknown adversary came on my third or fourth session at the water – a session being an evening stint of no more than four or five hours. I loved the channel at Harlesthorpe, a narrow strip of water running between a

Self-portrait. The artist, Brian Naylor, with a Harlesthorpe fish.

popular public bank and dense lily and reed beds. I looked on any stint on the channel as a real battle of wits because fish feeding there had seen it all before and tended to be a bundle of nerves when they were moving through the area.

I caught the first time I fished the channel, although I can't recall the weight of that first fish. I was fishing an experimental bait which certainly turned the carp on and I had the one fish and a great deal of indicator activity besides. On my second visit I had a common carp about a mile long. It weighed 14lb and gave me an epic scrap in the narrow confines of the strip of water I was fishing. It was a windy night and I can still hear the sound of the line singing to near breaking point while I tried to subdue the frantic common. At the time I was freelining big baits tight to the lilies and this second fish set off much too quickly for comfort. I knew that a really big fish would cause considerable problems given that sort of start and began to wonder if freelining made sense.

I was there again the following evening. My mate Trev was on the dam wall but he left mid-evening. This was September and it was getting dark at about 7.30 or 8 p.m. An hour after dark the moon emerged from behind the clouds and I thought that the brilliant moonlight would be the kiss of death to my prospects of catching. I sat and fretted, not daring to move my feet because of my proximity to the fish. I was a smoker at the time but the water was gin-clear so I didn't dare strike a match. I recall that I was so uptight about unnatural noises and vibration that I was even fishing with the buzzers switched off. There are moments you remember more clearly than others, and 9.55 brought an indelible one.

I had just cautiously poured a cup of coffee from the flask when the silver-paper indicator scraped off the spear and steadily climbed the eighteen inches or so to the butt ring. I was fishing bail arm on, anti-reverse off and my right hand went for the butt while my left hand was clapped over the face of the spool. I struck hard into something solid. Because of the lilies there was nowhere for the fish to go, so as far as I was concerned it was going nowhere. My unseen adversary had other ideas, and went. My mind registered total disbelief as the rod tip was dragged slowly and relentlessly down towards the water and a huge bow wave bulged across the moon's reflection in the pads.

I didn't panic, but my mind couldn't cope with the unexpected. The rod was well on the way to being pointed and I just couldn't stop it happening. If I gave line the fish was through the pads and behind the reedbeds. My thoughts raced,

The artist's impression of a younger Tim Paisley with one of his channel fish.

but not quickly enough. Twelve-pound line, size 2 hook. I tried to hold, still not believing the slow-moving power that was dragging the tip down. I blew it. I was pointed, the line gave and I was shaken. I didn't know where to put myself. I've never reacted as badly to the loss of a fish before or since. I was totally *shattered* and it was almost ten months before I could get myself back on the water again.

I didn't know what it was. I'd heard no rumours of a monster in the water but that fish had made an impression on me and I went back for another crack at it. I didn't think it would fall for the big freelined bait again, and I definitely wanted it stationary, or moving very slowly, when I set the hook in it. How could I create a baited situation which would produce the type of take I needed to have a chance with the power of this fish?

I settled for a situation which would just take account of one fish at a time, a light scattering of small (damson sized) stiffish paste baits fished tight to the reeds or lilies. The hookbait was fished on a 9-inch heavy braided hooklength, casting weight being provided by a one- or two-swanshot link. The length of the hooklength was critical. Too short and there was a chance of bolting fish, and while there was a chance with a fish in the lilies the reeds were tackle wreckers and too sharp to risk even the toughest line on. Too long and there was a chance of bite-offs, or the fish starting to move quickly before an indication was given. Nine inches was guesswork but once the fish had confidence in the bait it worked out right. AJS antenna buzzers and plastic-ring isotope indicators fished on a drop of 12–18

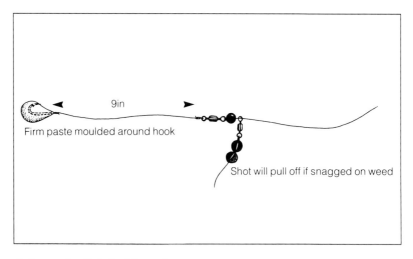

A 2 swanshot link for Channel carp.

inches completed the set-up. Short, alert sessions fed by coffee, but without cigarettes. It was in one of these sessions that I tried to drink a slug. It had crawled into the cup unobserved and had suffered having hot coffee poured all over it. I don't know which of us was most surprised.

Rods were of very soft action, 1¼–1½lb test curve, fishing bright-blue 15lb Sylcast. The tackle strength felt like overkill and when the going got tough I occasionally tackled up with 8lb line, then retackled with the heavy gear ten minutes after casting out. I kept telling myself that I was fishing for one fish and that when the moment came I had to be prepared.

I had a slow start, then the method began to work. One of the first fish came one July evening shortly after I'd had my tackle stolen for the first time. The fish weighed 19lb 7oz and was caught in broad daylight. My weighing sling must have been among the stolen tackle because we weighed the fish in the landing net, witnessed by thousands. We hoisted it up while I hastily explained that the figure shown would be a false one – but a small boy dashed off, proclaiming to the world that the mester had caught a 21½-pounder!

I averaged almost a fish a session after that, having some blank evenings, but having three fish on a couple of occasions. For the most part the takes were all slow lifts to the rod. I had no fish bolt on me, although one of the three-fish bags fell to striking one-inch twitches. My Jim-Gibbinson-inspired twitcher-hitting practice stood me in good stead that evening: wind up almost tight, tense the muscles of the hand holding the reel seating, and strike the second it buzzes. I had another nineteen (19lb 15oz and a bit), a glorious seventeen-plus linear, and a number of other fish in mid-doubles. The only fish I doubled up on was a plump scrapper of 9lb 12oz.

I went up to the water one Sunday evening in October. The last two anglers from the day session were just packing up – carp men – and we passed the time of evening. I held back from setting up because I was fishing a spot that no one else fished, and taking the better fish from there. It was in the channel, but opposite the boat-house reedbed, about half-way along, and I was beginning to think that the bigger fish lived in that reedbed. The further up the channel I went the smaller the stamp of fish I caught, which might have been only coincidence.

The last car left the car park and I set up stall. The swallows were gathering and the noise they made as they settled to roost in the reeds was deafening. As though a switch had been thrown it went quiet. It was overcast with no wind at all – not

The author fishing twitcher hitting style on the channel.

ideal conditions for the channel, but promising for all that. The familiar trap was laid – twenty small paste baits, ten around a hookbait of the same size, the other ten spread along the foot of the tall reeds. I was neither optimistic nor pessimistic. It was one of those evenings when you just enjoy being there carp fishing.

An hour into the waiting, maybe two hours, I heard the stems of the reeds across the channel from me rustle. It was a dark night, and pitch black against the foot of the reeds, but I couldn't see or hear any sign of a water bird, and there was no unfurling ripple. Carp? I'd never heard that rustling before, but then there was usually a breeze to mask the smaller night noises. I tensed, though, and was prepared for indicator movement – and it came straight away. The buzzer sounded and the LED on the left-hand buzzer head lit up. The indicator climbed halfway to the rod, then stopped. My hand was grasping the reel seat and my left hand was over the spool, but I hesitated because the indicator had stopped. The light was still on and the buzzer was still sounding, but again my mind didn't come up with the right answer quite quickly enough. It was eating the bait on the spot! I swept the rod back and everything went very solid.

I knew the routine by then. I'd had at least half a dozen fifteen-plus fish in similar circumstances and they had all wanted to go back into the reeds. When they weren't allowed to, they moved left or right in the channel and once that happened it was all down to patience and pressure. I hung on, but there was no movement either way. I was connected to a lump and felt – no, knew – that I'd hooked the fish I was after. The pressure didn't ease and I carefully started to stand up, with the intention of walking the fish away from the reeds. I was halfway up when the rod sprang straight and the swan link came skittering across the surface and struck the boards at my feet. I sat down, shaken but smiling. The bastard! The son of a gun! He'd done it again. I swung the end tackle into my left hand, expecting to find that I'd been bitten off. Not so. The point of the size 2 Lion d'Or was bent back against the shank, presumably mangled by my friend's bony throat teeth. He who hesitates . . .

I felt pleased with that summer's fishing, and the second loss didn't gut me half as much as the first one. I had fished to a plan and it had worked, give or take a couple of seconds.

9

Locating Hotspots

On some waters locating the carp is easier than on others. On almost all waters locating the hotspot in a swim is harder than locating the carp. Sensing and pinpointing the exact position in which the carp is most likely to accept a bait is one of the main keys to consistent carp catching. It is an aspect at which the natural carp anglers excel, possibly unwittingly, and over which we lesser mortals may struggle. If you are not a natural and can't anticipate the movement of the fish from your knowledge of the water, then you will have to work hard at that most tantalising aspect of presentation – just where the bait should be in the swim.

Anglers talk, and write, about carp location as though it is the answer to every carp-angling problem. I think this is a mistaken point of view. Year in, year out there has been no more frustrating water than Redmire Pool, but that is a three-acre water on which it is difficult *not* to locate carp. Finding fish and getting them to make a mistake and accept a hookbait are two very different propositions. That famous natural carp angler Jack Hilton had this to say about one of the swims at Redmire:

The first place they'd touch the bottom was under the willow in the '35' swim. There was one dead spot there, a real hotspot; it was no bigger than a foot across. I know it sounds funny but on a number of occasions I'd have a bait no more than a couple of feet away from that spot and the fish would be coming across, dipping down, doing their first little bubble there and my bait has been ignored. And yet I've moved the bait and got it to the exact spot and of course they've come diagonally across and sucked up whatever was there and you've had a take.

The spot he was talking about was less than two rod-lengths out from the bank, and he knew the swim well – but he still had problems getting the bait in exactly the right spot. How many times are those difficulties multiplied when the hotspot is

Jack Hilton, a very successful carp angler who gave up carp fishing in the mid-1970s.

further out into the lake, or you are fishing at extreme range? Precise bait placement can be very hit-and-miss in those circumstances.

I learned two early practical lessons on hotspots, both from well-known anglers. The lessons helped explain why successful anglers are successful: they are naturals, and they pay attention to detail. I have only seen Rod Hutchinson fish once, I think, and that was on his local Lido in Lincolnshire. I wasn't fishing but Rod explained something about the water to me while I was there. In the course of this he pointed out a localised hotspot halfway out to the island, a spot into which no one would ever dream of casting a bait unless they knew it had some significance. 'The carp usually dip down in that one spot as they come through,' Rod explained. As it happened, a carp did come through while I was there, and it did dip down in that precise spot. I never did quite understand why Rod didn't have a bait there! But imagine the waters you fish, the waters where you cannot observe fish because of coloured water, or distance problems. If you've got an island to go at the baits are usually tight there, six inches away. I used to fish that way at Snowberry Lake, and it often brought results; yet on the wood side of the water there was a stream bed halfway from the bank to the island and whenever I fished a particle, or seed, in the area of that bed I always had good results.

I watched Ritchie Macdonald fish at Longfield a number of years ago. I was still in his swim when he recast after landing a fish and he didn't ask me to leave, so I observed – which is slightly different from watching. Now, when you see anglers cast out on a gravel pit they often draw the end tackle back, and you can normally deduce why they are doing so – to position the end tackle where they want it in relation to a bar. Ritchie didn't draw back at all, and yet he recast a couple of times. As Longfield was his water at the time I didn't feel that I should ask him how he was positioning his bait, although I knew he must be casting to a known spot marked by a reflection on the water. I asked him about it some time later, after he had left Longfield, and he explained that he *was* casting to a reflection, and that it marked a small hump of rock which seemed to be on a patrol route. He took a March fish of 34lb from the spot while I was there. The consistent catchers of big fish are not successful through luck or by accident!

The big difference between the location of fish and the location of hotspots is an obvious one: the fish can often be observed in areas where they don't feed. If your bait and presentation are good enough, carp can sometimes be caught in

Cuttle Mill Fishery in the Midlands. By no means a difficult water, but bait placement can be all important here.

those areas, but the known – and unknown – hotspots are often feeding locations. Some feeding areas can cover a lot of ground; others may be very localised, and to get the best out of a swim you may have to pinpoint a hotspot of no more than a foot across. Whenever you cast out make a mental note of exactly where the bait hits the water and keep covering the spot if it brings results. If it doesn't, vary your casting. Try to visualise how, where and when the carp feed in the swim you are fishing, then try to locate a spot where the carp's defences are down and they will let themselves be caught.

Feeding areas, or localised feeding spots, are the most obvious hotspots to theorise about, but they are not always the most obvious to locate. On waters where the carp are strongly on baits almost anywhere in the lake might be a producing area, but that is rarely the case in practice. Waters where the carp have become dependent on baits are usually subject to considerable angling pressure, which leads to their feeding behaviour being directed to avoiding getting caught. On many waters of this type a vicious circle comes into effect. Initially, provided the bait is desirable enough, or the baiting situation alluring enough, or the presentation good enough, the carp can be caught without the angler resorting to any extremes in presentation or bait placement. But, as the pressure on the carp increases through their being caught – and on some waters subjected to repeated captures – a change in feeding attitudes occurs and productive areas are shunned or visited only with caution.

Another obvious hotspot, but pressure makes the fish nervous of easily identifiable, confined areas like The Gap on Darenth Tip Lake, pictured here.

John Lilley prepares to cast out on a Shropshire mere. Finding the hotspots on a water like this is very hit and miss; as a result, much of the fishing is done to markers and an artificial feeding area.

The carp appear to stop feeding on baits, but in fact they do not. What happens is that the caning they have received makes them particularly careful in identifying the hookbait. The surprise element becomes a necessity for consistent catching. The bait has to be better, presentation different and more efficient; the cast has to go further into areas where the carp haven't been caught before; baits against snags and margins have to be cast ever tighter to the 'safe' area. Then, as time goes by, *all* baits are cast to extreme range; the boaters and the swimmers place their baits ever tighter against the snags, or into them; particle situations are created at long range. *Extremes become the norm* until the surprise element disappears completely. What happens then? Angling takes over again and the vicious circle is complete. Subtler thinking has to replace merely reaching further out or further under. Margins under the angler's feet become productive again – because they are safe areas! Better baits replace irresistible smells. Lines are taken out of the clips and laid on the bottom. Efforts are made not to spook the carp before they have even encountered the baits, and the methods in use are honed to perfection.

Throughout this cycle there will be natural feeding spots which the carp know to be safe. It is the artificially created hotspots that will be subject to change. Part of the secret of carp fishing is *anticipating* what pressure will do to the fish and planning accordingly.

How do you set about locating the productive swims and the hotspots when you first visit a water you don't know? If the water is already being fished you will have to go to school on the other anglers to some extent, but think for yourself while you are observing what is going on. Resident anglers tend to fish on the basis of past experience and they are often the ones to miss out on the subtle changes that are taking place on their own water. Whenever you fish, have confidence in your own thinking and your own assessment of the water. You may be the next Rod Hutchinson in terms of carp location and their feeding spots, but to aspire to that standard you must believe in yourself, even when your thinking is at variance with everyone else's.

Finally, there is a form of location with which many carp anglers are familiar, but which is difficult to explain, and that is instinct. When I'm fishing a great deal I develop a sixth sense for carp location and bait placement. If I feel a strong impulse to fish differently from the way my mental calculations suggest, I *always* follow the impulse. It doesn't always result in success, but then neither does following the logical thought processes in swim selection and bait placement. On the other hand, being ruled by that gut feeling has brought me some good fish at times when I had no other reason for being where I was, or fishing the way I was fishing, apart from instinct.

For me this sixth sense operates only rarely. For the most part my efforts at carp location are the same as most other carp men's: I go to school on others; I observe, and move when necessary; I store knowledge and fish in accordance with where the fish should be in the prevailing conditions. Like many others, I prefer to fish with the wind in my face, but on some waters this preference is not justified. On some waters I can out-think the fish on bait placement; on others I struggle desperately to catch the occasional fish through good luck or persistence.

We all feel lost at times; we know we are getting it right and feel good at others. You will be no different from most other carp men if that is how you feel, but it is with location – more than any other aspect of carp fishing – that determination can mean the difference between success and failure.

10

Winter

by Bill Cottam

As far as winter fishing goes I have reached the situation where the mind is half willing but the flesh is very weak. Winter-carping enthusiasts keep telling me that I'm missing out – that the banks are quieter, the fish are at their biggest, and they feed just as avidly in the winter as they do in the summer. Occasionally I become convinced and talk myself into fishing the winter through, but these sorties into the unloved usually coincide with the lakes freezing over at Christmas and thawing out again on 15 March.

My friend Bill Cottam fishes the year through, including the winter and the close season – he would continue to fish for carp no matter what restrictions were placed on the practice by nature or authority. His enthusiasm for winter carping is such that I asked him to write a piece about it for the book. He came up with the following – eventually.

My first read through Bill's contribution made me realise what I lack to be a true winter carper – insanity. In the course of the second reading I became more impressed, and it occurred to me how pertinent to winter fishing are Dick Walker's words quoted above: 'It must matter tremendously'.

TP

Freezing Fog, Black Ice, Snow Flurries, and Occasional Carp

I don't think there is a water in the country where the carp don't go on feeding through the winter, but it doesn't necessarily follow that every water will respond favourably to winter fishing. There are exceptions, but if you stick to waters where the fish rely on anglers' baits, at least to some extent, as part of their diet you will increase your chances. Densely stocked waters with very little natural food in them will invariably be a better proposition than rich waters with relatively few fish per acre.

Give it careful thought and select the water for your winter campaign based on all the information at your disposal. Once you have chosen the water you are faced with the biggest problem of all – locating the fish and finding the *precise* areas and spots where they will feed. Finding these spots can be even more important in winter than it is in summer because the fish seem to be very reluctant to move far in their search for food. In fact at times you get the feeling that they have no intention of feeding until the bait is stuck under their nose. It is imperative that you find them and fish where they are. To add to the location problem, the carp very rarely show themselves in winter on the waters I fish. So where do you start on location?

The known productive swims are an obvious place, but be prepared for the fact that the feeding times may have changed: very often a 'night water' in summer will produce fish in the daylight in winter. If your lake has a wooded bank, a row of trees, or an island with overhanging trees, the fish may be there. Areas that aren't exposed to direct sunlight seem to be preferred, and can be very productive spots. Carp seem to prefer areas where the water temperature doesn't fluctuate too much in winter.

Winter: a heavy frost and a thin layer of ice.

Don't make the mistake of heading straight for the deep water. The fish may be there, but very often they are not. Look for areas with the highest oxygen content, because oxygen availability does seem to be an important winter consideration – inlets, outlets, under waterfalls and very shallow water, particularly during or after a high wind. A big percentage of my winter fishing is done in water three feet or less in depth. Over many winters of carping the only explanation I've been able to make for the apparently odd places the carp are in during the coldest water conditions is that they are seeking the most highly oxygenated water, so if all else fails base your guesswork on that.

I've been through all the various phases on bait but I'm now a firm believer in high-quality 'high nutritional value' (HNV) baits. I'm totally convinced that using them properly produces better long-term results at any time of the year, but especially from October onwards. In winter carp tend to be very lazy and seem to prefer food that will fulfil their nutritional requirement for the least amount of physical effort on their part. Good-quality baits are the answer.

Flavours I've found to be effective in winter include Rod Hutchinson's Maltrex, Nectar and Ultraspice, and Geoff Kemp's Green Zing, all at 2 millilitres (ml) per pound of bait. I've never found it necessary to increase the flavour level in the

Overnight snow and a Christmas card effect in this fine picture by Steve Corbett.

colder months, and if you are using good baits it is as well not to anyway – but some of my friends do believe that upping the flavour level does improve their results. Until recently I had always steered clear of natural oils in winter but a couple of years ago we started experimenting with a natural, sweet emulsifier, with exceptional results. Successful oil/flavour and emulsifier combinations have included 8 drops of bergamot oil with 2 ml of Martin Kowal's ethyl-alcohol-based Strawberry Jam flavour, and 8 drops of clove oil with 2 ml of Richworth Quava. Tim and I have made this emulsifier available through Nutrabaits.

One of the biggest secrets behind consistently catching carp in winter is the assessment of the amount of bait to have in the swim at any one time. If I've got a bait established I don't hesitate to apply the bait to summer and autumn levels, but without a going bait I'll tend to have about thirty free offerings around the hookbait and top up after each fish or clear sign of action. Presentation is governed by the type of feeding situation you are trying to create, and you may need to experiment with various lengths of hooklink to get the fish to give you a clear indication. I rarely fish clipped up tight in winter now, and on some waters I'm prepared to strike at any unexplained sound from the buzzers or movement of the indicator.

Presentation does tend to be dictated by the degree to which the bait is established. If I'm baiting fairly heavily with a going bait, I use a braided hooklength with a single bait mounted tight to the hook. My hookbaits are usually neutral-buoyancy in this situation. I'm hoping to get the fish moving round the swim picking up baits at random; looking for a degree of preoccupation, or confident feeding.

If I'm baiting lightly with a bait that isn't established I'm hoping for pick-ups on the curiosity value of the bait, and at least one rod will be fished with the intention of drawing attention to the hookbait. PVA stringers are useful for doing this, as are pop-ups, double baits, or a bait that is totally different in smell and colour from the other baits in the swim. This creates a high curiosity interest and a couple of years ago brought me five fish during a winter's morning when everyone else on the lake was blanking. Because there are days when the fish aren't inclined to move, constant recasting with one rod can be a very useful winter tactic. Recast every hour or so, and if you aren't getting action in one area cast somewhere else.

Like most other people, I used to think that the best days for carp fishing in winter were relatively mild days, and that if a spell of warm weather was on the way the chances of catching

Lee Jackson, a Kent angler who has had some marvellous winter results.

would be much better. I look at things slightly differently now. After studying my results I firmly believe that constant temperatures, no matter how cold, are far more important than mild conditions. It seems as though carp need time to acclimatise before they will really get their heads down. Strange things happen in winter and you can get some very funny days . . .

★   ★   ★

Freezing fog, black ice and heavy snow flurries – not to mention the now inevitable five miles of roadworks – meant that the journey took almost twice as long as usual. We pulled into the lane leading down to the lake just as dawn was breaking. The sight that met us as we peered through the half-light was what I expected – a bank-to-bank sheet of ice. Notwithstanding various suggestions from Mark as to how we could clear enough of the ice away to fish, we were forced to accept that the lake was totally unfishable, and would remain so for some time.

Mark doesn't get as much time on the bank as he would like

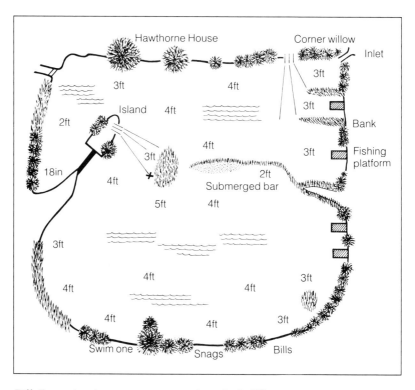

Bill Cottam's winter water – approximately 1–1½ acres.

so the prospect of three days fishing being snatched away from him was biting deep. He said nothing as we walked back to the car but I got the distinct impression that I was expected to suggest something. I did – a trip to the nearest café – but Mark desperately wanted to fish. Realistically, there were two alternatives – the River Trent (it rarely freezes) or a large dawn-to-dusk day fishery at North Muskham, about fifteen miles away. The Trent didn't really appeal to either of us so we headed for North Muskham, hoping that by some miracle the lake wouldn't be totally frozen.

I couldn't believe what was happening. It was half past eight in the morning, with freezing fog everywhere, and we were driving round the countryside desperately trying to find somewhere to fish for carp. Mark's enthusiasm was revived by the weather forecast predicting temperatures to rise to +1°C by mid-morning and the wind to increase by afternoon. I was still fancying the café.

We pulled into the lakeside car park and the expression on Mark's face said it all – we were fishing! About a third of the lake was frozen but the rest was clear, apart from a little ice in the margins. We set up in adjoining swims, cast about 70 yards to a known feeding area and sat back. We had been on the move all morning and it wasn't until we sat down that we realised just

Bill's usual set-up, plus a thick layer of frost and a frozen up water!

79

how cold it actually was. We were going through the motions and the chances of catching were *nil* as far as I was concerned.

The forecast was right and by 12.30 the water was clear. Mark came round for a coffee and talked me into returning to our original venue in the hope that some of the ice had cleared there. Back we went. The return journey was much less hazardous, the black ice and fog having almost cleared. Back at the original water some of the ice had cleared, and two swims were fishable. Within the hour we were set up and fishing. If it hadn't been for Mark's enthusiasm we wouldn't have been there, and even with it I was wavering.

We were fishing – again – but we were still going through the motions as far as I was concerned. The water was small, snaggy and a good winter prospect in the right conditions. These did not feel like the right conditions. To make matters worse, Mark had claimed the Corner Willow, a swim with two very obvious feeding areas under overhanging trees – a prime winter swim. I'd been forced into the only other fishable swim – on the island. My area of clear water was barely big enough for me to get three baits into, but I managed to squeeze them on to a sandy plateau, just short of some snags. I rigged all three rods with 8-inch braided bolt rigs, two baits being fished tight to the bottom and the third with a pop-up 2 inches off the bottom. This bait was balanced exactly to a small shot. Even in those conditions with a going bait I would have put a full mix out, but without the bait established I settled for about twenty free offerings.

By late afternoon the sun had disappeared behind the trees and the wind had dropped completely. Conditions looked worse than ever. The temperature had fallen another couple of degrees and the ice that was already covering 70 per cent of the lake was beginning to creep slowly back into the areas we were fishing.

I sat on the bed-chair with the sleeping bag over my legs and stared at the lines already thick with frost, wondering how long it would be before they would be frozen in. Mark appeared, walking gingerly across the icy bridge that led to the island. He was clutching a mammoth pack of beefburgers and a packet of cheese slices. Things were looking up; it was feeding time. The frying-pan went on and the smell of burgers soon drifted across the lake.

Mark was just about to do his Egon Ronay bit with the sandwiches when the right-hand Optonic signalled a drop-back bite. I frantically wound down to the fish and managed to catch up with it as it came off the plateau. Fortunately, the fish kited to the left away from the ice and I was able to play it in the open water. Mark did the honours with the net and on parting the mesh informed me that it was the leather, a fish that had eluded us for five seasons. My reaction was a mixture of surprise, delight and disbelief. As I tried desperately to warm my hands, Mark weighed the long-sought carp at 15lb 7oz. The light was fading fast so the fish was photographed with the flash before being slipped back into the icy water.

I rebaited with another suspended boilie and recast to the same spot. As the terminal tackle hit the water I heard it smash through the thin layer of ice that was forming over the plateau. The bobbin was set, the line clipped at the butt and the frying-pan went back on.

The burger and cheese sandwiches were followed by coffee and a chat about the day's events. Mark stopped in mid-sentence and pointed to the rods. The right-hand bait had again been picked up and the rod was bouncing in the rests. The rod tip had been plunged into the water when I tightened down after recasting and the water had frozen in the rings. Two turns

Five layers of clothing and the end of a five-year wait. Bill with the leather.

of the reel handle snapped the line out of the rings and a firm strike had the fish crashing through the icy surface towards the snags. Side strain just managed to steer the fish in front of the snags but it took much longer to subdue than normal; I had to keep the rod tip underwater most of the time so I could play the fish beneath the ice. After what seemed like hours, but was probably more like fifteen minutes, the fish was ready for the net – and once again Mark did the honours. The fish was a recognisable beautifully conditioned mirror weighing just under seventeen pounds. It made up an extraordinary winter brace from a far from prolific water in a little under half an hour in near-impossible conditions.

I tried to recast to the same spot but instead of going through the ice the terminal tackle slid along the surface of it. Ninety per cent of the lake was now frozen. The chances of landing another fish through the ice were remote so the other two baits were wound in and I turned in for the night. Mark carried on fishing as he still had a small area of clear water in front of him.

I crawled into the bag feeling a bit guilty. If it hadn't been for Mark's insistence I wouldn't even have fished, never mind caught a brace of good doubles. He got his reward in the shape of an energetic common of 7lb which he got me out of bed to land at nine o'clock. I had to smash a channel through the ice to

A beautiful Pete Springate study of Redmire Pool in winter.

net that fish. We went back to bed and slept the night through, both having caught on a day when you wouldn't turn a dog out.

★   ★   ★

If you are a newcomer to winter fishing, particularly session fishing, don't underestimate how harsh our winters can be, especially by the water, where the coldness is exaggerated. Take advantage of some of the excellent equipment offered for sale by the tackle dealers these days. Invest in a thermal one-piece suit, a pair of thermal boots, a good set of waterproofs and a warm sleeping bag (it is advisable to use two sleeping bags unless you have a very-good-quality one).

Be prepared for the length and coldness of the nights. In the depths of winter it is dark for seventeen hours out of the twenty-four. Make every effort to ensure that your stint on the bank is as comfortable as possible. Take plenty to eat and drink; you'll enjoy it a lot more.

Finally, although there may be long periods of inactivity don't fall into the 'they're not having it' trap. Don't assume that because you aren't getting action the fish aren't feeding. Be determined to catch, no matter what the conditions. Be persistent and keep fishing. Be positive, otherwise you are wasting your time going. The harder you try and the more you put into it the greater your chances of reaping the rich rewards that winter carping undoubtedly has to offer.

11

A Thing of Beauty
by Brian Garner

During the summer and early autumn a number of carp had been caught from the water. These fish had fallen to a variety of methods, and from various areas of the lake – but no one could really work out *why* they had caught. It was all a bit hit and miss and catching was something of a lottery.

At about nine acres this well-known Midlands estate lake is reputed to hold in the region of a hundred fish. The majority are commons, many of them growing fish already into the lower and upper twenties. The lake also contains a few big mirrors, the largest – and probably the biggest fish in the water – being a mirror of just over 30lb.

I had fished from the end of August, throughout September and into the middle of October with no action whatsoever. During these fish-free weeks I had started to formulate a plan of action in my mind which I hoped would get me in among some of those beautiful commons I had seen caught from the lake.

The lake is triangular, the southern end being the dam. Members are allowed to fish anywhere except from the dam wall. One side of the lake is known as The Meadow, from which the members have total access to the fish. The opposite bank, known as The Boards, consists of wooden fishing platforms and a walkway stretching two-thirds of the length of the lake. The remaining third of this bank consists of overhanging trees and a bed of rushes which stretch as far as the dam wall. This corner of the lake is inaccessible to the angler and I felt that it created a natural holding area because of its inaccessibility. The snaggy, weedy environment would obviously be an attractive, safe haven for the carp.

Some anglers had been fishing this safe area by wading down to the snags in chest waders either from the end platform or from the corner of the dam, and positioning the baits where it suited them. The method had produced fish but I felt that the wading detracted from the achievement of the capture of these

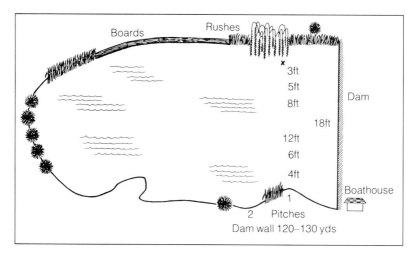

Brian's winter water – approximately 9 acres.

fish. But how else was it possible to fish this productive safe area?

The only alternative to wading was to fish from the meadow opposite and cast to the hotspot. It would mean a huge cast, but I was confident I could achieve this using the right equipment. I tackled the problem with 12-foot Tricast long-range rods of 2½lb test curve. Reels were Cardinal 55s loaded with 8lb BS main line and a 15lb shock leader to withstand the force of the fierce casting. Terminal tackle consisted of 18 inches of anti-tangle tubing with a 10lb BS Dacron hooklength tied through the eye of a size 6 Kamatsu to a 1-inch hair. The necessary casting weight was achieved by means of a 3oz Zipp lead. Bait was a high nutritional value base mix which I had used for the previous two years, the attractor being an emulsified oil/synthetic flavour combination which I had full confidence in. As a rule I introduced a full 10oz mix of the bait on each visit through the autumn so by the time I caught something I had put in well over two thousand baits.

Presentation of the bait was a simple 2-inch suspended rig, carefully balanced to the weight of the anchor shot, fished on a 15-inch hooklength. Buoyancy was achieved by means of a polystyrene insert – I prefer this method to cooking or microwaving the baits. Once the bait was established I felt sure that a single suspended bait cast to the fish in the safe area would do the trick without the introduction of further loose feed into that corner of the dam.

Towards the end of October I began to put my plan into

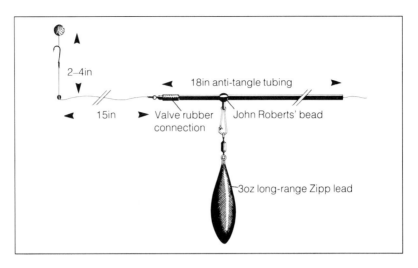

2–4in

18in anti-tangle tubing

15in

Valve rubber
connection

John Roberts' bead

3oz long-range Zipp lead

Brian's set-up.

action, and from the beginning of November I consistently
averaged a fish per session – and what fish! The best was a truly
breathtaking common which weighed 27lb 3oz.

It was early December and I had managed to get a Friday off
work. The weather was mild and the southerly winds were
pushing into the dam wall when I arrived on the water on the
Thursday afternoon. Prospects looked good and I was eager to
get the baits in position before darkness crept in. Getting the
baits out was the priority and when that was achieved I set up
my pitch. Once all that is done all you can do is wait and hope.

During the night the wind gradually increased in strength but
I was secure and warm and eventually fell asleep. I woke next
morning to the sound of rain lashing down on the bivvy; the
pitch was awash but my confidence was still high. Up to that
time the fish I'd caught had been hooked in darkness but I felt
hopeful of catching in daylight in those wild conditions. I'd just
decided to move my pitch further back out of the mud when
the left-hand Optonic sounded its shrill warning. A run! I
picked up the rod, wound down and set the hook. I could
instantly feel the power in the fish, the rod tip giving massive
bumps. The fish seemed intent on dragging the rod out of my
hand.

The line was high out of the water, cutting across the surface
and down into the murky depths. Great vortices were breaking
surface where the fish was slowly ploughing along, trying to
burrow deep into the silt. She stopped suddenly and I managed
to gain some line, but as suddenly she was off again, still a long

*Brian with a beautiful common of 27lb plus from the water described
in the story.*

way out and kiting towards the margin down to my left. I tried
to turn her but she would have none of it.

By now the fish was getting perilously close to the margin.
'Turn, you bugger,' I shouted out in my panic – and to my
amazement she did as I commanded. She was in open water
now, out in front of me, and I felt a lot more confident. By this
time I was drenched to the skin, my right arm had begun to go
numb and my heartbeat was racing fiercely.

I had my first glimpse of the fish as she flashed by in the deep,
clear water in front of me, showing a long, golden flank. The
fish was tiring, but so was I. The net was already sunk, waiting;
I had to get this right first time. She came up under pressure and
slowly, inch by agonising inch, came in over the net. In she
went first time. I lifted the net out of the water and gently laid
the fish on the grass. She lay there panting with exertion, a
long, golden common carp – a thing of beauty, and almost
flawless.

I photographed her and lost no time in returning the carp to
the water, savouring my last glimpse of her as she glided
swiftly away into her crystal-clear environment. I stayed out on
the point for a while, just looking out across the water,
knowing that I'd had an experience which would stay with me
for the rest of my life.

12

The Business End

Most avoidable carp-fishing disasters result from a flaw in the last two or three feet in the set-up. Any lost fish is a disaster; it means that you've just wasted a lot of time, and it might have been the fish of the session, the fish of the season, or the fish of a lifetime. My end tackle is always designed to cope with the situation in which I'm fishing and I try to eliminate all risk. However prudent you are, things can still go wrong, but always do all you can to reduce chance to an absolute minimum.

I frequently swap experiences with other carp men regarding hook types, lines, and so on, and I would suggest that you do the same. It is a commercial age and the carp market sees new products every day. It is difficult to know which of the new items can be relied upon until the collective carp-world tackle-test system has had the chance to appraise a new product.

This chapter is about getting the best out of your end tackle. I've used a variety of hooks, lines, swivels and bombs and I've

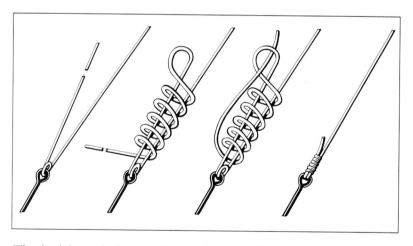

The clinch knot, the best that I know for braided lines, and the knot I've used all the time since I learned it from a Jim Gibbinson article in the mid-1970s.

had the odd disaster with gear that should not have let me down. If you are 100 per cent happy with the tackle you are using then don't be influenced by what follows. But if you are new to carp fishing, or are having problems, what follows may help.

Swivels, Knots and Leads

I'll start with something simple – leger stops. When anglers first turn to carp fishing they are often afraid of knots, thinking that they weaken the set-up. They don't, but leger stops do because they crush the line. Don't ever use a leger stop in a carp fishing set-up; use a swivel. I've shown three perfectly reliable knots here which are more than adequate, even with braided line. I've been using swivel stops for twelve years now and I've *never* had a breakage at the swivel. I can recall what a pain tackling up was when I was first having to tie three knots in the end tackle, but I soon got used to it. In those twelve years I've had just one hook knot go on me, and that was when I was using an unsuitable prestretched nylon line as a hooklength. You have to tie a hook on and that is potentially the weakest point in the set-up. You must master a reliable knot for carp fishing so practise one until you have complete confidence in it.

If you are using a running lead make sure that you protect the main-line swivel knot with a bead, and ensure that the bead will

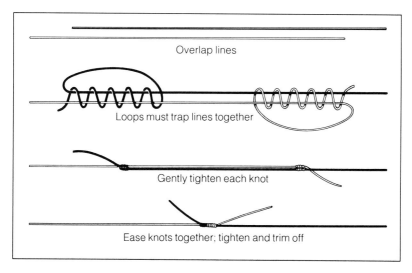

Overlap lines

Loops must trap lines together

Gently tighten each knot

Ease knots together; tighten and trim off

Double grinner knot for connecting two lines together.

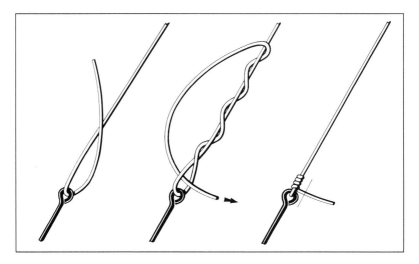

The blood knot – widely used but not 100 per cent reliable with some braided lines.

fit over the knot. Most beads have too fine a hole so simply put a scissor point into the hole and bore it out until it does fit over the knot. I've had numerous rethinks on leads over the years. I'm currently using end-on leads in conjunction with 2 – 3 feet of anti-tangle tubing in much of my fishing. If you don't use end-on bombs, and you like using a link swivel (a set-up I've used a great deal and still use in some situations), cover the link completely with rubber or shrink tubing to stop the braided hooklength blowing back round it.

I use Berkley swivels at the join of the reel line and hooklength. I don't like tying knots on the diamond-eye swivels, and I once had a swivel that wasn't a Berkley break on me when I was playing a fish!

If your set-up is such that the lead can swing against the hooklength when you are playing a fish, protect the area of the hook length at risk with rubber tubing.

Hooklengths

I've been using braided lıne for over five years and I'm a bit of a slave to it. I have had reports that some anglers are getting better results with mono now, so it may be wise to keep an open mind on the subject and find out for yourself. It may depend on how heavy you have to fish. Once you go above 10lb BS I can see braided having the edge. Below 10lb BS it will

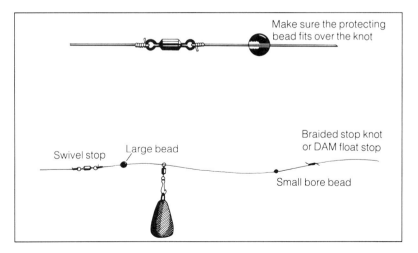

*A swivel as a leger stop arrangement, with a bead to protect the
swivel knot.*

*This 20lb common is one of a brace of twenties taken on the bomb on
the end of the line presentation with a 4-inch braided hook length.
The fish were silt feeders and were caught within an hour of each
other.*

*A 23lb mirror, the other half of the brace. I feel that silt feeders are
more likely to fall to short hook lengths than fish in some other types
of waters.*

depend on the fineness and reliability of the braided you are
using. A number of us use a couple of industrial threads which
break at 8–10lb and are very fine. I won't use them for heavy
work, or where abrasion on snags is a hazard, but they are
terrific for all but the most fraught situations.

There are some good braided lines available for the heavy
work. I've used Masterbraid for three seasons, on and off, and
I've very impressed by it. I've also found Black Spider to be
totally reliable, and very supple. I like the look and feel of the
Berkley braided that Terry Eustace sells but I haven't used it.

There are other braideds available but the hooklength is such
a vital area that I'm going to restrict my recommendations to
personal experience with them. I'm happiest with Masterbraid
in 10, 12 or 15lb BS and I've got total confidence in it with both
eyed and spade-end hooks.

Hooks

Ten years ago there were the Richard Walker carp hooks, solder-blobbed low-water salmon hooks, and the eyed version of the Au Lion d'Or carp hooks. Now there are more specialist hooks on the market than I've had carp. I keep having my opinions about hooks changed by differing angling circumstances and by experience. Hooks have a massive influence on your carp fishing. They are the only indispensable item of tackle and your hook, more than any other factor, decides whether you will land your fish or not. It is not my experience that all the hooks currently available are equally effective, and some are a gimmicky waste of time. I used to think that any carp hook would do the job, but I no longer think that; I don't even think that one type of hook can be right for all carp-fishing presentations.

Provided you can set the hook to the bend I think that most hooks will hold in most situations. Problems increase as pressured fish become warier and hookholds become less than adequate. With the bare-hook presentations, we tend to use hooks which are just strong enough to cope with the angling situation we find ourselves in. But the effectiveness of a hook which just pricks the fish is based on different considerations from those influencing a hook set to the bend.

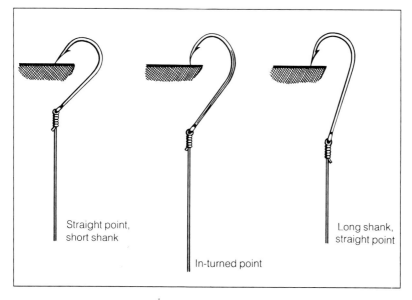

The angle of pull on the point of different types of hooks.

The drawings show the position of a hook when it has just made penetration. With the straight-pointed short-shanked hook, the angle between the pull up the line and the direction of penetration is about 30 degrees. When full pressure is applied to the point it may be forced open and lose its grip. This can happen on the strike, immediately after hooking, if the angler is having to hit and hold, and near the net; the pressure on the hook increases either when the fish comes up in the water or as it comes under the rod tip, when the playing action becomes more of a lift than a pull. I think that this pull across the point, rather than along it, is exaggerated where very short (3–6-inch) hooklengths are used. Friends and I have had very strong hooks straighten or open out when we've been using short hook-lengths, particularly fishing the bomb on the end of the line. The angler can exert a great deal of pressure on the hook on this set-up and change the position of the hook on the strike. I now always use in-turned points with short hooklengths.

Hook (b) is a hook with an in-turned point – the shape of the Lion d'Ors, the Rod Hutchinson carp hooks and the Gamakatsus. I use spade-end Lion d'Ors for much of my fishing now, flattening the barb almost to the hook and sharpening the hook to a needle point. A long time ago, and I'm not sure where it was, I read a comment by Rod Hutchinson to the effect that hookholds were hit-and-miss, and that he thought a hook worked its way in during the course of the fight. At the time I couldn't see what he was getting at, and dismissed it as a load of cobblers. I can now see that he was absolutely right, as usual, and that he was probably referring to the in-turned-point hooks at the time.

I prefer spade-end hooks for a couple of reasons. I use the Domhoff knot (I don't know who Mr Domhoff was but he must have had a very tortured mind) and I manipulate the knot so that the hooklength runs over the middle of the front of the spade. I then superglue it. I think this positioning and supergluing makes the knot 100 per cent safe and helps make the best use of the shape of the point.

The longer the shank on a straight-point hook, as in the Richard Walker carp hook, the more direct the pull on the straight point. There don't seem to be many long-shanked hooks around now, and I don't think most carp men are enthusiastic about them anyway, but it may be that for a straight-point hook to match the strength of the in-turned points it will have to be longer in the shank than many of the straight-point hooks are currently.

I carry a hook sharpener with me and I use it frequently. I

A beautiful mid-twenty caught in the middle of a hard week's stint.

have used the chemically sharpened carbon hooks, but I prefer a hook I sharpen myself. I can certainly make the hooks I use sharper than any artificially sharpened hook, and I've got the injuries to the end of my thumb as evidence.

If you've got a good hooking/landing record don't change a thing. If you haven't got problems don't look for them – confidence in the tackle you are using is a major factor in putting fish on the bank. Balancing baits makes the use of heavier hooks a practicable proposition, but there will be situations in which I'll go back to my favourite Drennan Specimens (green packet) or Super Specialists. Stick with what you know and understand, but if there are possible problems ahead – and the situation does alter as the fish get spookier – it is as well to be forewarned.

Finally, do test your end tackle. Hook it up to a fence, or the mother-in-law, and give it some welly. Just after you've hooked a fish is no time to find out that all is not well.

Come to Daddy! Ken Townley with Big Daddy.

Nick Elliott with a magnificent prize, a winter thirty caught under the rod tip on a hard southern water in the severest of conditions.

Carp Society's General Secretary, Baz Griffiths, with a fine south west mirror of 26lb.

This beautiful mirror carp was still fighting when the picture was taken by Dave Preston, and then required half an hour's nursing when it was returned to the water.

Ritchie Macdonald had a 34lb March fish from a not very obvious hotspot.

Rod Hutchinson, a natural at pin-pointing the hotspots.

Dave with one of his many 20lb+ fish.

Brian with the biggest of his fish which came on the long chuck: a superb common of over 27lb.

Productive margin: the centre bank at Cuttle Mill. I had a number of fish from a single bait fished a foot from the bottom of this bank on an otherwise unproductive sort of day.

Kent carp man Mark Summers with a fine fish taken on a heavily pre-baited HNV bait.

A superb study of a twenty-plus carp taking chum mixers. (Picture by Martin Herbertson of Hampshire.)

Greg looking well pleased with Redmire Pool's Raspberry at 24lb 8oz. This magnificent fish is known to be over fifty years old.

Brian Garner's beautiful common.

The warm glow of the sun in the chill of a winter's dawn.

Selby angler Julian Cundiff with a lovely scattered mirror from Hull and District's Tilery Water.

13

Tackle

Apart from the business end, which has just been considered, the major indispensable tackle items are rods, reels, line and, for long sessions particularly, buzzers. I've asked all the contributors to the book to give some indication of the tackle they use. This is not to suggest that you should do as they do, but carp anglers do tend to go to school on each other's experiences and the most suitable rods, reels and line tend to finish up in common usage. There are fashions and trends but for the most part a certain brand of a tackle item becomes widely used in carp fishing because it is tried and tested and found to be both most suitable and most reliable.

Carp fishing is an expanding leisure pursuit and the market is expanding with it. New products keep appearing – and some of them disappear because they just aren't good enough. Give some thought to tackle selection before you spend your precious cash.

Rods

Selecting the right rod is a headache. There is a wide range to choose from and where carbon is selected your rods will represent your largest single financial outlay. This is an area you really need to discuss with a specialist rod or tackle dealer, or an experienced carp angler. Failing that, the following advice is very basic, but it may help.

All reputable carp rods are 'strong', so don't confuse stiffness with strength. Carp rods fall into three rough categories and can be assessed in terms of test curve. The test curve of a rod is the weight which will pull the rod into a 90 degree curve when hung from the tip. The test curve value, however, gives no indication of where the action lies in a rod so a further designation states whether the action is 'through' (or compound) or 'tip' (fast taper). In other words, you can have two rods of the same test curve but with very different actions and a

The author's set-up during a Cuttle Mill session: AJS buzzers, 2¼lb TC North Western Specimen rods, light indicators. I'm not fishing fixed lead here; I want every sign of interest in the bait to register an indication so I can get a quick idea of the effectiveness of the bait and presentation.

*A 2lb TC Alan Brown Spiraflex under compression, casting a
2¹/₂oz, lead and small bait eighty yards.*

very different feel. In a fast-taper rod the action is mostly in the
top section of the rod; in a through–action rod it is more evenly
distributed. The table shown is a starting point for understanding the characteristics of the various rod categories.

Classification	Test Curve	Range	Action
soft	1–1½lb	margin –30 yards	through
medium	1½–2lb	30–90 yards	through or fast taper
stiff	2–3lb	70 yards upwards	fast taper or through

Anything outside the 1½–2¼lb test-curve range is a very specialist rod. Select the softest-actioned rod which will perform the functions you require of it in the circumstances in which you will be fishing. The softer the rod (the lower the test curve) the nicer it will be to play fish on and the greater margin of error it will provide when you are playing a fish under the rod tip. With carp rods the difficulty is balancing action and power, which is why you will see even some long-range rods described as 'through-action'.

In terms of casting ability there is a rough-and-ready formula which states that casting weight is approximately equivalent to one sixteenth of the rod's test curve. In other words, a rod with a test curve of 2lb is designed to cast a weight of 2oz. The formula was more accurate with glass than it tends to be with carbon. The best carbon rods are a marvellous blend of suppleness and strength and will normally cast a greater weight than their test curve rating suggests.

I've used a wide range of glass rods in my carp fishing but since 1981, when carbon started to take over, I've used carbon rods of 2–2¼lb test curve for most of my carp fishing. I'm currently using a range of North Western carbon-kevlar rods and I'm extremely happy with them. That's not to suggest that they are necessarily better than the rods available from the many very reputable rod makers in the specialist world (some of whom are using North Western blanks anyway), but they are very reliable rods and I can recommend them without reservation. As an all-round rod the 12-foot, 2¼lb test-curve Specimen is one of the most pleasing rods I've handled. It's a very long caster and surprisingly sensitive for playing fish on.

Don't be afraid to ask for your own specifications for any carp rod you buy. I prefer cork handles and always ask for them, and I think that the standard ringing on many of the rods intended for long casting is of poor design. If you are likely to

How prepared are you? This fine action shot is of Bill using a beach caster to create a particle bed eighty yards out.

The beach caster unwinding.

do much long-range fishing the ring specification shown (originally designed by Rod Hutchinson) gives a good compromise between casting and angling considerations.

Reels

Nearly all my carp fishing has been done with Mitchell reels and I'm currently using a pair of 810s. Eventually the reel market will settle down but at the moment it is suffering a wind of change. At one time almost everyone used Mitchells, then ABU Cardinal 55s became *the* carp-fishing reel. Manufacture of this fine reel was discontinued some time ago, although new models still seem to be available and they are prized items on the second-hand market. The newer Mitchell models are not as popular as the original 300, 410 and 810 ranges; I think this is mainly because the line-lay on some of the newer models isn't as good as on the originals. There was an indication that the Browning reels would fill the void left by the discontinuation of the manufacture of the Cardinals but there were faults with the original Brownings and the market has yet to acquire confidence in the revamped version. The Shimano reels are highly spoken of, and widely used, and while they are not yet as firmly established as the Mitchells and Cardinals they are considered by many to be *the* long-range reel at the moment.

What are you looking for in a reel for carp fishing? Well, something that is well made – and in this respect some of the new Japanese imports just don't inspire total confidence. You want a spool with good line capacity, a deep spool (front to back) as an aid to long casting and a reliable, smooth line-laying action for the same reason. Ideally you want a reliable clutch for safety, particularly if you do much of your fishing close in. I rarely use the clutch when I'm playing a fish, relying on the feel of using the backwind, but a carefully set clutch does give you the confidence to set the hook firmly in any circumstances, and at any range. Again, talk to other carp men, or a specialist dealer who stocks a range of reels before you commit yourself.

Line

Line is another tackle item with which experienced carp men tend to play safe and rely on the time-proven brands rather than risk losing fish on one of the new brands that appear annually. When I started carp fishing I was told that carp men used

Maxima in the 6–8lb BS range and Sylcast in the higher breaking strains. Being a 'free thinker' there was no way I was going to be brainwashed into using what everyone else was using just for the sake of it and I set about discovering the wisdom of the advice the hard way. Some disasters later (over a three- or four-year period), I settled for using . . . Maxima in strains up to 8lb and Sylcast Sorrel in the higher strains. You cannot be too careful with line and I've had unhappy experiences with a number of lines of perfectly respectable brand names.

On the other hand, I do think that the line market is changing for the better and I know a number of carp men who now swear by brands other than the two I have mentioned. Over the last two or three years I have heard good reports of Brent, Rod Hutchinson's Specimen line, Ultima and Daiwa, so these lines are well worth having a look at. Do approach the use of any line with considerable caution. There is a lot of waiting involved in carp fishing and when you do pick up the rod to set the hook your line must act as you want it to, and you are entitled to expect it to.

Over the last eight years I have had just one bad experience with line and I dismissed it as just one of those things – which it turned out to be. The advice I was given originally turned out to be uncannily accurate and it says much for the consistency of the lines concerned that the advice was given over twelve years ago. I use Maxima in the 6–8lb range, but find this a little bit too springy above 8lb. I'm happy with Sylcast Sorrel in 9, 11 and 15lb, but have had some bad spools of 6 and 8lb. If I'd stuck with the original advice I was given on line I would have saved myself a great deal of heartache and landed more carp than I have done.

One final point on line. If you are fishing at any sort of range always buy your line in bulk spools. Spooling up with connected 100-metre spools is very risky because the line invariably receives minor damage at the join of the spools.

Buzzers

The only other tackle item I'm going to cover is buzzers. They are not absolutely essential for short-session fishing, but they are for the longer sessions when you are sleeping on the rods. Even on day sessions buzzers are a great help because they enable you to watch for carp and enjoy the natural world around you – and there's always the possibility that you will nod off after getting up in the early hours of the morning. If you are like me it's a certainty you will nod off!

There are two types of buzzers: the antenna, which operates through the line tightening against a vertical antenna and closing two contacts together; and the wheel buzzer, which is triggered by the line passing over and rotating a wheel, which in turn breaks an electronic beam. In my opinion the best antenna buzzer is the AJS and the best wheel model the Optonic, or Delkim. Since the Delkim is a conversion of the Optonic original these two models operate in the same way; any variation in performance is due to the degree of efficiency of the electrical systems used.

There are advantages and disadvantages in both the wheel and the antenna systems. Where all indications are full runs, or positive movements of the indicator, the Optonic/Delkim systems are ideal. But where the carp are becoming finicky and reluctant to move with the bait there is a case to be made for the use of antennas. An antenna buzzer will register a tightening of the line, and will also give an indication when the line stays tight by continuing to buzz. With Optonics these small

Bill's set-up for fishing over the particle bed. Spiraflex 2lb TC rods, Optonics (Delkim conversions), indicators fished at the top of the needles and line butt clipped. He's fishing fixed lead and must make provision for drop back indications.

Be prepared: we live in an unpredictable climate. This lovely shot is of Ken Townley's friend Steve Westbury playing a fish in a badly timed rainstorm.

movements may not register at all, or may only result in a single insignificant-seeming beep.

On the other hand, the Optonic systems are the best for registering drop-back indications, which can be quite common with heavy fixed leads. I've experimented with the AJS alarms for drop-backs but it is difficult to achieve an audible indication.

I do think that the wheel systems have become so fashionable that they are now being used irrespective of angling consider-ations. In the past I've caught carp on long buzzes from antenna alarms with no movement of the indicator, and as I'm experimenting with both types of system at the moment I hope I will catch the odd bonus fish that way this season. A screaming Optonic is an exciting carp-fishing sound but when the runs dry up the angler's end of the carp fishing set-up has to be given almost as much consideration as the business end.

Carp tackle is expensive, so mistakes can be costly. Take the trouble to go to one of the specialist fishing tackle dealers if you aren't quite sure which version of an item of tackle will best suit your needs. Go in when business is quiet and the dealer, or the specialist salesman, has time to talk to you. Alternatively, go to a Carp Society or a British Carp Study Group or Carp Anglers Association conference to see what's available. There is so much first-class equipment on the market that investing in cheap, inadequate or unsuitable tackle can easily be avoided with a little effort.

14

Tangles

There is nothing worse than reeling in after a blank night and finding that the end tackle is tangled. (There are many far worse things but at the time it happens you tend to forget all the others.)

It is important to ensure that when you cast out the end tackle lies in the swim as you want it to. Reach for the anti-tangle tubing? Possibly, but even when you are using anti-tangle tubing you have to give your tackle some thought, and I'm not sure that anti-tangle tubing is the automatic answer anyway.

I think that most tangles occur because the bait is off the hook. We didn't get tangles before the hair. During the 1983–4 season I wasn't using tubing and I didn't use stringers all the time. I tied the braided hair to the hook with water-soluble PVA string before every cast, retying when I had to recast, and I didn't have one single tangle throughout the season.

This lovely seventeen pounder fell to a stringer fished on a long braided hooklength well away from the baited area.

Bomb link with anti-tangle tubing. Encase link in rubber tubing for safety.

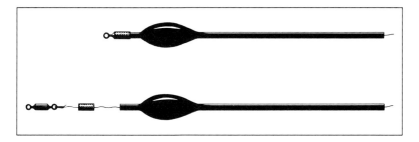

Bomb and anti-tangle tubing, semi-fixed by rubber tubing fitted over the swivel and the end of the tubing.

Let's look at tubing. It serves two purposes: one is to prevent tangles; the other is to mask the main line on waters where it is felt that fish are starting to spook off line, or spook away from certain familiar types of line. Far-fetched? I don't think so. I would think that in the underwater environment everything has a smell of its own. On the heavily pressured gravel pits abrasion-resistant snag leaders are essential, because of the bars, and for years a high percentage of the lines that have been used on these waters will have terminated in tough Sylcast shock or snag leaders. I've no conclusive evidence on carp spooking off lines, only a shared opinion with other anglers that it happens and a couple of experiences that gave food for thought. At a time when I had fish feeding on a bait, but couldn't arrive at the correct presentation to put fish on the bank, I fished a rod with tubing against one without. *All* the indicator action came to the rod with the tubing. Over a two-week period on the same pressured water five fish came out. All fell to anglers using line

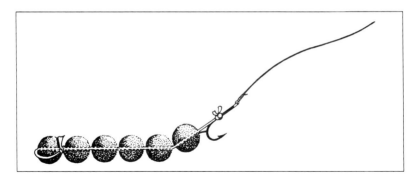

A Rod Hutchinson invention, the PVA 'Stringer'. Thread the PVA through the free offerings and the hookbait and tie round the shank of the hook. The PVA dissolves after the baits have been cast into position.

A big twenty from a southern gravel pit. This fish fell to a stringer presentation. It took me nine casts to get the end tackle where I wanted it, which is a lot of messing around when you are using stringers. Sometimes the result is worth the effort.

other than 11 or 15lb Sylcast. Not only are those facts inconclusive, they are downright vague, but getting it right is an accumulation of plusses, and on some waters it just isn't worth risking a possible minus.

Some anti-tangle tubing floats, which means that it stands up from the bomb if you don't weight it, or aren't fishing tightly clipped lines. We use 1½ millimetre single-core copper-wire tubing with the core stripped out, which sinks. If you are on a water where you think line masking might be important, use the longest length of tubing you can safely cast out, irrespective of the length of the hooklength (subject to the tubing being longer than the hooklength, of course).

I think that end-on leads are far superior to leads which hang down; if you use the latter make sure that it really is tangle-proof by covering the link in soft rubber tubing. End-on leads used in conjunction with a length of very heavy line (40lb BS) also effectively eliminate tangles. Do your own tests on this before you really commit yourself; at the time of writing results are satisfactory, but not 100 per cent conclusive.

I fish PVA stringers a great deal and I've never ever had a tangle after casting out a PVA stringer. I use the stringer as shown when I want it to act as an anti-tangle device as well as an angling tactic.

Anti-tangle tubing is effective, and it can be essential, but at times it can be a liability. It adds weight and air resistance and can cut down on distance when you want to fish at extreme range. Be aware of the alternatives and have the confidence to use them when they are required.

15

Bait

Your bait must be as good as it needs to be to enable you to catch the fish you are fishing for. I'm tempted to end this chapter there, while I'm ahead. I don't think anyone can disagree with that first sentence – and there are almost as many outlooks on bait in the carp world as there are baits!

In bait terms 'as good as it needs to be' is vague; it is intended to be. In carp fishing, bait and presentation must be looked at together. A bait that is good enough in terms of attraction can fail because it is fished as a soft paste; you may be fishing the right particle bait, but introducing too much, or too little, to get the best out of it; you may be fishing the best nutritional bait on a water but it can fail to produce the results you want if it is up against an established nutritional bait and you don't introduce enough bait to compete with the *availability* of the other bait; a perfectly good protein bait with too high a level of attractors can fail in the long term.

Bait is food, but it is also an angling principle, which is why

This small-water 15lb fish fell to tiger nuts presented on a bolt rig. The end tackle was cast out in a PVA bag with about thirty nuts in it.

hard baits are now used in place of the soft pastes which were used in the sixties and seventies. On any given day a carp can be caught by the most attractive bait, or the most effective baiting situation operating on that day, but over a period of time, particularly where an angler is fishing one water for a season, the best results can be expected with a food bait that the carp accepts as part of its diet.

Bait is an exercise in logic and practical application. Consider the carp, then consider the bait and the way in which you are going to have to apply it to achieve the result you want. Carp can be caught for one of a number of reasons; they are principles we all subconsciously work round in our angling, even if we don't always fully define to ourselves our reasons for adopting a certain approach. Here's another mnemonic: padac.

A carp can be

Preoccupied with . . .
Attracted by . . .
Dependent on . . .
Annoyed with . . .
Curious about . . . a bait.

There is undoubtedly some overlap in those categories, and the fourth principle may need some explaining, but padac summarises the main principles of bait and its application.

Preoccupation is aimed at through the introduction of a large enough quantity of (usually small) food items to make the carp forget the possibility of danger and make a mistake in the course of its feeding. With this method you are trying to take advantage of the carp's natural greed and create a feeding situation similar to the carp's natural feeding. Size of bait is important, as are quantity, placement, and, in the longer term, food value. Seeds, particles, mini-boilies, chopped-up boiled-paste baits (paste particles), maggots, boilies, chopped-up luncheon meat – any food will do. The more individual food items there are per given quantity of food the greater the potential for achieving preoccupation.

Attraction can be instant, and very temporary, or it can take longer to work and extend over a period of time. A good attractor in a poor bait will catch carp, but it usually has a limited life; but a limited number of attractors do seem to go on working over a period of time irrespective of the food value of the bait. Carp have sensors and they respond to certain 'smells', or chemical cues. Flavours, essences, oils, amino acids, esters, yeasts – a wide range of substances will attract carp and good results can be achieved if the bait is made so attractive that the

A fine big double. This was one of four fish in a day from a 'night only' water! I thought I'd got the bait spot on, but the attractor level was too high and the bait didn't catch another fish until it was modified.

carp has got to pick it up. There is a woman to make a fool of any man, and a bait to make a fool of any carp. I found the woman, I'm still looking for the bait. As it can be with the opposite sex, the stronger the initial attraction the stronger the possibility of the relationship being a short-lived one. Don't be surprised if a bait that catches the first day you use it draws a blank thereafter. It sounds like a contradiction but the very fact that a bait is instant can mean that the attractor level is too high for the bait to be edible, and that the carp won't find it acceptable as a food after it has been eaten. Don't bait up with an attractor bait of low food value. The food value has to be balanced against the attractor level to achieve lasting results. Get it right and you will find that love at first sight can sometimes be the real thing.

Dependency on a bait is achieved by the steady application of a bait of high food value. Bait is food and the better the food the more readily the carp will go on accepting it over a period of time. Protein and high nutritional value baits are a science in their own right, and a fascinating one to many, but I don't think this is an area to be discussed in depth in a book of this type. I've included a couple of recipes for those who are interested, and I'll make one or two points about the use of nutritional baits from the angling aspect.

Kent angler Bill Walford with a 30lb plus fish caught on a steadily baited nutritional bait flavoured with one drop of garlic oil.

1.   You are not baiting up to persuade the carp to pick the bait up. They do that from the off. Baiting up is done to give the fish the confidence to accept the bait as a food supply and pick it up when it is attached to a hooklength. There is a world of difference between what carp will eat and what they will get caught on.

2.   The better the bait the less of it the carp will need to eat. Although you will need to keep a steady supply of the bait going into the water over a period of time, it may not pay to have too much in your swim while you are fishing. If the carp will need to eat, say, only ten of your baits in a feeding spell, and you are only going to get half a dozen fish through the swim over a feeding period, then you may struggle if you automatically fire out a full mix. This is a mistake I've made on a number of occasions and it was only through observing that fine carp angler from Crayford, Alan Smith, applying his nutritional bait that I realised I was applying a perfectly good bait badly. I'd got too much good bait in the swim at a time when the fish weren't feeding heavily and they could afford to be selective – and not take the hookbait.

3.   For your nutritional bait to work properly the carp must look on it as a food supply, and therefore *availability* is important. You are competing with the carp's other foods, both natural and artificial. Get the bait right in the first place, being careful not to detract from the food value by overdoing the attractors, then make sure that the carp get a regular supply of it. Keep 'em coming back for more; create a dependence; *believe* in what you are doing – belief is half the battle with nutritional baits because they take time to reach full effectiveness.

Annoyance with a bait sounds odd, but I'm sure it happens. As with the next category, the annoyance factor tends to work best with single baits, but it does go further than that. I have observed some curious reactions to baits over the years and there was a time when I was far more inventive than I seem to be now. The modern carp-fishing methods have stifled original thinking, I'm sure, and it's only when I reflect on how I achieved some of my past results that I fully realise the truth of that.

On some waters we used to fish floating baits in splendid isolation out in the middle of the pool, and getting a carp to take one in its mouth was a real battle of wits. Softish baits they would smash off the hook, then eat the bits. But some days they would persist until they'd broken up the bait, then ignore the pieces! That struck me as odd, and I learned that if I could find a bait that was hard enough to survive indefinitely they would eventually take it. I got the impression that they were taking it just to get rid of it.

On a scorching hot day at Snowberry Lake when there was absolutely nothing happening one solitary carp gradually became increasingly obsessed with my large wholemeal crust stuck out in the middle. It would not leave it alone and kept coming back to it, rolling on it, smacking it with its tail and generally abusing it. I counted, and the fish made fourteen separate attacks on that crust over a period of two hours in conditions so hopeless that it never once occurred to me that it might take it. Eventually it did, though – a totally isolated bit of action on a very uncarpy day.

I saw this happen on a number of occasions after that and began to play on this annoyance factor. It's a game that's as hard on the angler's nerves as it seems to be on the carp's, because you often have to leave the bait out there far longer than you want to. It can work when all else is failing, though, and make an acceptable bait out of one the carp wouldn't normally make a mistake with.

Going on from that a bit, I learned to play on this annoyance/curiosity aspect and discovered that a variation which also redeemed the odd hopeless day was a combination of two baits together – of different types, or colours. Again this started off as a real desperation tactic and began with a piece of white crust fished hard against a piece of brown. Until this variation went out the carp really didn't want to know but they couldn't leave the combined baits alone and I had a succession of fish. I've since employed the same tactic successfully with different-flavoured, different-coloured suspended baits.

Curiosity feeding probably overlaps the annoyance factor at times – and attraction too, I suppose – but I've seen captures which I could only put down to the need to know what the source of smell was. Genuine curiosity feeders seem to be few and far between, in the sense that they represent a low percentage of the fish in some waters, but it can be a welcome percentage when the going gets tough. The technique is to fish one different bait over a bed of baits or just off the baited area, or a hookbait of one smell with a stringer of the main bait. It is a practicable tactic but, if you do get it to work, accept it for the method it is. When you catch a fish this way there is a temptation to change the smell of your main bait to the smell that caught the fish. It wasn't necessarily the smell that caught; it was the need to know, the curiosity. As the French say, '*Vive la différence*'; or, as Rod Hutchinson put it, 'Try something

*Alan Smith from Kent. I've learned a great deal from his very
effective application of quality HNV baits.*

Have the courage of your convictions. This 18lb plus common helped convince me I was on the right lines with a bait change that I believed was right but didn't have full confidence in.

different'. I'm not sure either reference was to carp fishing but it's a principle that's worth remembering.

The five elements of padac each owe something to the bait employed and as much to the method of application and presentation. I have caught carp on all these methods and in the process my thinking on bait has changed over the years.

To start with it was a question of coming up with anything that would help me catch a carp; my approach to bait had no pattern to it. I think it's fair to say that in the seventies the majority of carp anglers didn't give a great deal of thought to *why* a bait caught carp, it was enough that something was rumoured to do so. Many of you will be happy with a pack of boilies from your local tackle shop – and why not? At the other end of the scale, some of you would have liked to see more about the theory of bait here. The beauty of bait lies in the eye of the beholder. Whatever your approach to bait, learn to apply it to your best advantage and acquire confidence and belief in that approach.

This book is concerned with the catching of carp, rather than big carp, but I'll make one further point about bait. Many anglers find it difficult to adjust their approach from trying to catch just any carp to trying to catch the bigger carp from a water. It is all too easy to dismiss other anglers' big-fish captures as luck and convince yourself that you are unlucky. Well, nearly all my bigger fish have fallen to high nutritional value baits with a good attractor or distinctive label fished on a very simple presentation. On some waters the biggest fish are the most curious and are the first to fall to a new smell; on other waters the big fish have to have confidence in a good food bait before they can be caught. To my mind the most reliable approach to catching the better fish is to apply a good food bait over a period of time and hope to get all the fish in the water accepting it. Once you have a working bait of your own you can focus all your angling knowledge and skills towards trapping the fish you are after.

Don't underestimate the value of a good bait. Confidence and good thinking come from using a bait that you know the carp will pick up. The more enthusiastic the carp are about the bait – the more they *want* it – the greater your chances will be. There is far more to carp fishing than bait but in any given set of circumstances, all other things being equal, the more a carp wants your bait the more likely you are to catch it.

I'll close this chapter by listing the baits with which I've caught carp; those with which I've had most success are italicised. Seed and particle baits are listed, followed by some recipes which may serve as a basis for a successful bait for the reader.

Successful Baits

Maggots, worms, worm-maggot cocktail, bread flake, *crust, floater cake,* trout pellet paste, *Fish & Liver Kit-e-Kat and PYM,* Pond Flakes and PYM, *maize, maples,* sweetcorn, luncheon meat, *Bacon Grill, protein paste with Minamino, tiger nuts* Minglefruit plus casein (the only commercial bait preparation I've used), and a succession of *protein, nutritional value* and high nutritional value baits based on Fred Wilton's original theories and my own interpretation of them.

Seeds

Prepare by soaking.

Hemp
Tares
Dari seed (red or white)
Oat groats
Buckwheat
Rape
Millet
Sago

Particles

Soak and boil – except sweetcorn.

Sweetcorn
Tiger nuts
Maize
Black-eyed beans
Chick peas
Peanuts (dangerous when used excessively)
Hazelnuts
Various beans
Various peas

Attractor Baits

Ingredients Semolina, ground rice, soya flour, wheat gluten, ground Weetabix, Layers' Mash – plus eggs to mix and attractors and sweetener as required.

Sample recipes

10 oz semolina	8 oz semolina
6 oz soya flour	4 oz soya flour
5 ml molasses	2 oz robin red
5 ml liquid liver	1 oz Vitmin
10 ml Minamino	1 oz casilan
5 ml scopex	10 ml olive oil
¼ ml cinnamon oil	2 ml Guava
Eggs to bind	2 ml mango
Roll out, boil till hard.	2 ml molasses
	¼ ml bergamot oil

Nutritional Baits

Sample recipes

Protein bait	*HNV bait*
2 oz Lactalbumen	2oz Lactalbumen
2oz Caseinate	2oz egg albumen
2oz Soya Isolate	2oz Bengers
1oz Vitmin	1oz Davina protein food
1oz egg albumen	1oz Vitmin
1oz wheat gluten	8oz Rennet casein
3oz Rennet casein	15ml olive oil
¼ teaspoon Cajoler	⅓ml clove oil
10ml olive oil	2ml Guava (Richworth)
1ml geranium oil	Eggs to bind (approx. 6 size 2s).
Eggs to bind.	Stand paste in plastic bag for one
Roll out, boil for approx. 60	hour; roll out and boil for 50
seconds. Use within 24 hours of	seconds. Use within 24 hours of
making, or thawing if frozen.	making, or thawing if frozen.

It's important to understand that protein and HNV baits are *principles*, as opposed to exact recipes. You are putting together a high food value bait and the recipes shown here are just examples of long-term baits which the carp will respond to and

This was the pantry. As George Bernard Shaw said 'You've got to be single to be single minded.'

go on eating over a long period of time. It is important that the level of attraction be kept low as some attractors work on a short-term basis and don't make a good long-term bait additive.

If you want to put together a protein or HNV bait of your own, as many anglers do, make a pound mix, keeping an exact note of the ingredients used. Make the egg-plus-attractors mix to half quantities, then add the powder until the right consistency of paste is achieved. Weigh the remaining powder to discover exactly how much you have used in the half mix; this will enable you to calculate precise levels for future mixes.

16

Big Daddy

by Ken Townley

I guess I'm like most other people in that I hold a very special affection for the water where I caught my first twenty-pound carp. Mine came from Salamander Lake in Cornwall and weighed 20lb 3oz; I've been in love with the place ever since. The love affair dates back some ten years now and began with the capture of a bristling little leather of just over 8lb. This was followed by a big bruiser of a fish which came to be known as 'Big Daddy'. As I watched him grow over the years this fish became the personification (if that's the right word for a carp) of Salamander.

In the early days the fishing was hard and particles in the edge, fished on the hook, was *the* method. Then along came Lenny Middleton's brain-child, the hair, and we all had a field day. Of course it couldn't last and over the last three years or so the place has become really hard. I regard any fish which comes out as a gift from the gods as these post-hair fish are wise beyond their years. In fact I've tended to drift off in search of challenges on possibly easier waters, but from time to time Salamander has called me back.

One cold, snow-peppered winter's day I happened to be walking the banks of the lake and chanced across a mate of mine who staggered me with the news that he'd had Big Daddy at 24lb 12oz. Well, that was enough for me and for the rest of that chilly winter of 1983 I spent many a session at Salamander, determined to put this great fish on the bank. It was not to be. To rub salt into the wound, the fish came out again during the first week of the following season at 24lb 14oz – and didn't make another mistake for the remainder of the year.

I spent some time on the water towards the end of 1985 but although I caught more than my share of good fish I couldn't get near Big Daddy. Finally, one sultry, oppressive July day a fish picked up my three-bait stringer fished in glorious isolation close to the margins, and after a tremendous fight lasting some

Ken returning a College Reservoir fish of 22lb plus.

fifteen minutes I drew the fish towards the net – and the hook knot went! The fish lay for a few seconds, unaware that freedom was his for the taking, and it was Big Daddy. He looked huge – certainly big enough to harden my resolve to try again.

During the close season of 1987 I started a baiting programme and from mid-May onwards spent many hours looking for fish and baiting up. Eventually I managed to concentrate some of the fish in a small bay, hedged by a thick cover of willow trees. There were plenty of fish to be seen, but Big Daddy was not among them. Then, at last, when I was beginning to despair of ever finding him, I spotted him on the fringe of his feeding companions. Slowly and cautiously, he inched towards the baits, gulped a great mouthful down, then bolted, not to return that day.

As the opening week approached I upped the amount of bait going in, using two, sometimes three 1lb mixes daily. They were loving it – and, yes, Big Daddy was in there with the rest of them. It was clear that the bait was going well, so I'll say a bit about the bait I was using. For a couple of seasons I'd been using a high nutritional value bait and at this time I was modifying it, testing out a couple of ingredients and a liquid. The base mix is given at the end of the chapter. The Bengers and the Davina contain specific protein-digesting and protein-splitting enzymes – trypsin in Bengers and bromelain in Davina. In use the latter enzyme requires an acidic trigger

The Townleys session fishing. Carol is cooking the breakfast while Ken does the hard work of taking the pictures!

(among others) to achieve its purpose and this was the reason for including the *low-level* organic acid.

I was convinced that the wily old fish of Salamander were not going to be fooled by the boilie-buzzer-bivvy approach. I thought that if I was to stand any chance at all I'd need to do something different in terms of bait size and presentation. I was sure that Big Daddy would be wary of standard-size baits, so I made mine up as mini-shapes, produced by using the smallest (8mm) Gardner rolling table then just cutting the long, thin sausages into very small pieces. This gave me about 1,500 mini-baits to a pound mix and a 10–15 seconds scalding was all they needed to skin them.

All this prebaiting and bait making was *very* hard work, and also pretty costly, but my determination to catch the big fish was running wild.

At first the small fish in the water found the bait much to their liking but once the carp moved in the others didn't get a look-in. There was no doubting the attraction of the bait and eventually I had all the fish in the water feeding on it. Seeing two dozen good fish with their heads down devouring a mix in about twenty minutes was a very satisfying sight.

I felt confident that the most effective approach would be stalking with a single rod, using a soft compound rod and float tactics. After all, I'd already got them feeding in the edge; I

Carol catches her share of the fish and her personal best stands at over 20lb. Here she cradles a College double figure fish.

could watch them picking up bait so long sessions seemed unsuitable. I was so confident that I was going to have Big Daddy that I wrote to Tim during the close season and told him that I was going to catch this big fish. Then, just before the opening of the season, disaster struck. I had to go away from home on a job for a couple of weeks, so that was that.

Back from the big city, I shot up to Salamander at the first opportunity and was happy to see the place almost deserted; there were just a couple of anglers on the water. They reported no action at all and told me that the other lads had moved on to other waters, feeling that Salamander was not going to produce. The water was as clear as crystal and my prebaited swim was free. Would the fish still come into the margins after the early season pressure? Would they still want my bait?

Creeping down to the water's edge, I chucked in several handfuls of minis and sat back, nerves all on edge. The fish didn't show and after a couple of hours I was beginning to get worried – they had been on it like a shot on previous occasions. At last, about half past three in the afternoon, the first big fish drifted into the swim. I hadn't even wet a line, not wanting to risk spooking the fish, but gradually, as several fish turned up, I felt I could risk putting the float out.

I turned away from the water to bait the end rig and when I turned back there he was – Big Daddy in all his glory. My heart rate went through the roof and my legs turned to jelly; I could hear the blood thumping in my ears. He looked huge. I swung the tackle out and edged the float right up to the bank under the

Ken's set-up in the margins – simple, but very effective.

willows. The line went down to a single swan shot and then via the small swivel to a size 8 barbless Mustad 34021 hook. A string of mini-baits was tied to the eye of the hook with sewing cotton. I could plainly see the little cluster of baits as they lay on the bottom in just a couple of feet of water.

The great fish approached the end tackle and tilted down, and I saw the hookbait disappear into his cavernous mouth. I struck and he was away, through the nearest weedbed in seconds and emerging on the other side of it leaving severed weed stems in his wake. Once through the weed he turned sharp left and, with the line still trailing through the weeds, plunged into the overhanging branches of the left-hand willow tree – where he stuck fast.

Paul had heard the commotion and crept in to see what was happening. 'Hold this a second,' I shouted to him, thrusting the rod into his hands. I started to strip off and was down to my pants when Paul quietly muttered, 'He's free.'

I grabbed the rod and watched as the line swept away from the tree-line and out into the open water. Now I felt more confident, but suddenly he came shooting in again and once more snagged me up in the same tree. Again the rod was passed over, and again I started to go in for him – and once more the fish came free. (If you ever need a guy to get a fish out of the snags for you, Paul's your man!) This time I made sure the fish would give me no further cause for a dip and after a terrific scrap under the tip I eased him into the waiting net. He was mine.

We got out the scales and I watched with great delight as they registered 26lb 14oz – my second heaviest fish, and one I'd been after for over three and a half years. I gave a whoop of delight and chucked my sling up in the air, where it got caught in the nearest willow! I didn't care a hoot. Big Daddy had succumbed to all my patient and determined effort.

What a wonderful prize. I shall never forget it.

The Bait

7oz Rennet casein	2g Bankside Cajoler
3oz egg albumin	½ml N–butyric acid
2oz Bengers	15ml Minamino
1oz Davina body build	15ml liquid liver
1oz SBS Vitmin	6 No 2 eggs
2oz Lactalbumin	

17

Scratching the Surface
by Brian Skoyles

The carp nervously raised its dorsal fin until its leading edge just broke the surface, sending tiny ripples radiating out. With a gentle, almost nonchalant twist of the tail the fish changed direction to position itself for the next group of Mixers as they floated against the margin weed.

From where I stood I could see every minute detail – the mouth opening and extending, the tiny whirlpool as another Mixer disappeared. Nothing else existed – time standing still. Only this tiny corner of the pond mattered. My own bait was next in line. Any second now the cramp, the stings, would all be worth it.

For hours I had fed the area, catapulting free offerings into open water so that the gentle wind could drift them into the margins at my feet. For hours I'd been standing, hidden in the taller reeds, watching as the fish, at first indifferent and nervous, had gradually become relaxed, interested and hungry. I'd watched as first one Mixer then another and another had been taken.

The cast had been made into open water and allowed to drift back to its natural position. Next in line. The fish gave another gentle flick of its tail and for a moment we seemed to stare each other out. What was it thinking? Could it see me there? Could it sense my quickening pulse and thudding heart? It moved again, closing on my bait. Go on, any second now.

Bee---ee---ep!

Oh damn! Where am I? When did those lights change? When did those cars in front move off? The bloke behind isn't too happy.

For me surface fishing has a magic that I find very difficult to describe. It's often very personal. You become involved not only with the surroundings, you also seem to become intensely involved with the fish. Perhaps it's because you can see the fish,

A mid-twenty cautiously feeding on Chum Mixers.

can sense the tension, understand its caution. Of all the different styles and types of carp fishing, stalking surface-feeding fish remains for me the ultimate. From the moment I load the car it takes over. Anticipation of things new, memories of highlights past. Twenty-mile journeys take for ever, and traffic lights . . .

Consistency in surface fishing requires three things: commitment, patience and versatility. It's not just a case of banging out a surface bait because it's hot and nothing's happening on the bottom. Certainly, on some days you'll catch fish that way but on others you'll be missing out on so much.

Anyone interested in surface fishing needs to think in three main areas: presentation, bait, and watercraft.

Presentation

To be effective, the bait – whatever it is – must be presented to the fish in such a way that it is fooled into thinking it is safe, or at least worth the risk. This means that it must behave as closely as possible to a free bait. On the surface this can involve problems of drift, bait buoyancy, line visibility and hook visibility.

It is very rare to find the waters that we fish completely still, so it is likely that any free offerings we put out on the surface are going to move about. This can be an advantage on some days, on others a right pain in the neck. On balance I prefer a breeze of some sort, as it means that baits can be drifted over

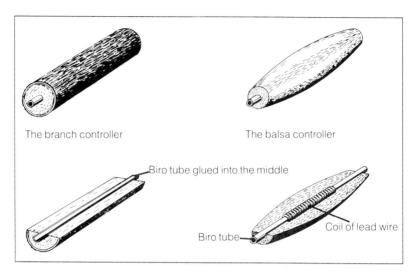

The branch controller

The balsa controller

Biro tube glued into the middle

Biro tube

Coil of lead wire

Controllers.

fish rather than having to wait for fish to come to the baits.

The hard part is to make the hookbait drift in a similar fashion to the free baits. In calm or very light wind conditions hookbaits tend to drift slower than free baits and in stronger winds race past all comers with gay abandon.

To help correct this I use controllers of two main types, as illustrated. The first type is made from small sections of tree branch, of which there are always plenty around after a good gale. A good average size is approximately 1 inch in diameter by 2 inches in length. They are easily drilled out, and I glue a length of biro tube in the drilled hole to help protect the line. An alternative is to use balsa dowel with a biro tube and lead insert.

These controllers are used mainly on the calmer days when their surface bulk and buoyancy are an advantage in helping to drift baits into position. It is not uncommon with this type of controller to keep the rod tip high so that the line drag is reduced as much as possible. The natural wood controllers are usually very buoyant and move readily; the lead-insert controllers can be adjusted during manufacture to be more or less buoyant as required. I tend to carry a range of sizes and degrees of buoyancy so that I can match drift speed with the free baits as closely as possible.

The second type of controller has been nicknamed the dumb-bell, and it's easy to see why. This controller has proved very successful in conditions where greater control and stability

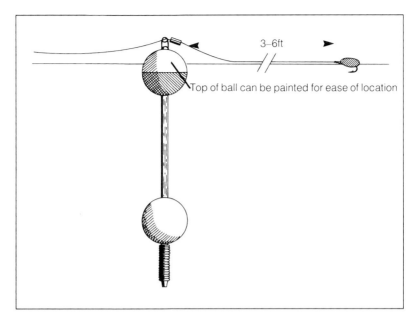

Top of ball can be painted for ease of location

3–6ft

The dumb-bell in use.

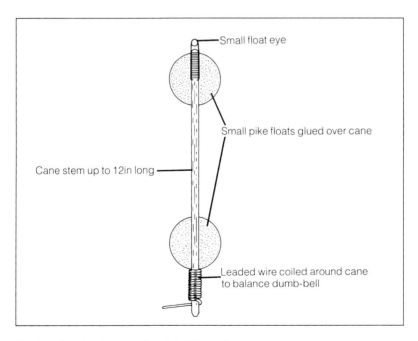

Small float eye

Small pike floats glued over cane

Cane stem up to 12in long

Leaded wire coiled around cane to balance dumb-bell

Section showing how the dumb-bell is made.

of the hookbait are required. The idea is to have the bulk of the weight well down in the water, which helps with mending line, and so on. Again I carry a range of sizes for varying conditions. With a range of the controllers illustrated you are giving yourself a better chance of success.

The types of controller already mentioned are best suited to a combination of relatively clear water, no more than moderate wind and short to moderate range fishing (about 60 yards maximum). In more snaggy conditions I prefer to use the snags as a means of trapping both my free baits and hookbait. One of my favourite ways of doing this is illustrated. Again I've used a small section of tree branch, this time with a garden staple hammered into the end. When the device is cast to the weedbed and allowed to snag, the bait can be held in position as shown. The rotten link shown in close-up is advisable as the controller can become a liability once the fish is on in very snaggy conditions. I don't mind losing them as they are very cheap to make and environmentally safe.

In stronger winds or at long range it can become necessary to resort to anchored rigs. The two versions I use are illustrated. The first is best suited to shallow water whereas the second can

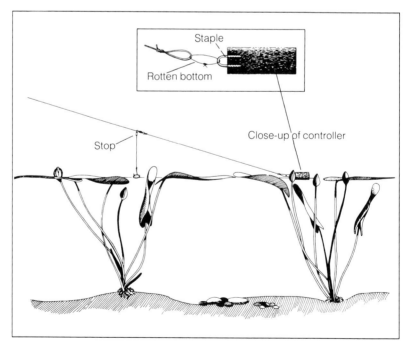

A snag rig.

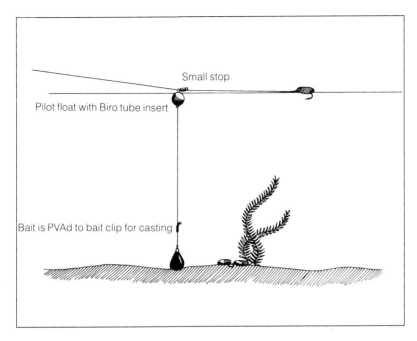

Anchored bait rig for shallow water.

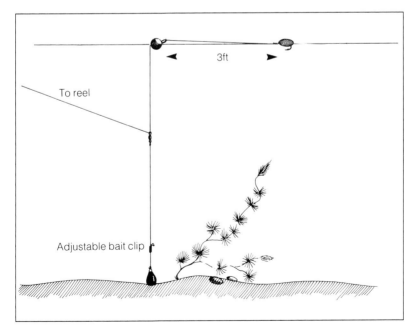

Anchored bait rig for deeper water.

135

be used in much deeper water. The purpose of the sea angler's bait clip and the PVA'd hook is to avoid tangles on the cast.

Overall, the key word in all this is versatility. The aim is to present a bait that the carp will accept as safe. The advantage of fishing on top is that you can see if you're getting it right. Look closely at the way your bait moves and compare it with the free offerings. Check how it rides in the water. Does the hook make it look different? Does it balance in a different way from loose baits? Most important of all, what do the fish think? Your bait is in the middle of thirty or forty free offerings; fish move in and mop them up, leaving yours. That means that you've got some work to do. Don't just accept it – try to solve it.

There is no such thing as the perfect rig, but you can often find a presentation that will work on the day if you are prepared to experiment and adapt to the conditions. Be prepared to experiment at home with hooking arrangements, making hooks buoyant, and so on. You get funny looks when visitors call and you are sitting with a large bowl of water on your knee playing with soggy dog biscuits, but the results can be worth it.

One example of being adaptable is illustrated. It's one of my favourite stalking rigs and it has caught fish from some hard surface waters. It's only suitable for very close-range work but it's great fun to use. I first used it when I was stalking some fish which were under a large overhanging tree. I had been drifting baits under it for a long time and judging by the noises and the cloopings the carp were having a party. Every now and then a mouth would be seen just short of the edge of the leaves but the

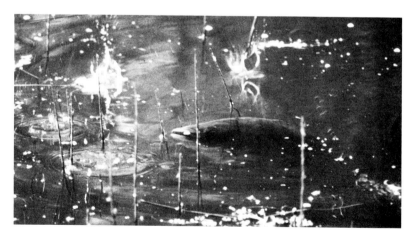

No caution here. This carp can't get enough of the bait and is feeding on the Mixers as they are thrown in.

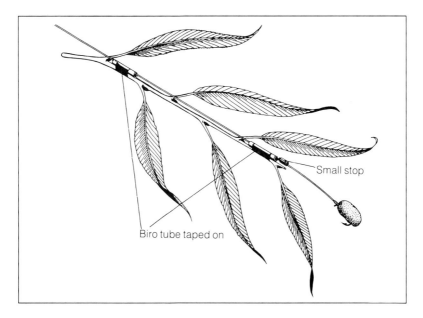

Have tree, will travel!

fish would not venture out into the open water. I didn't want to allow a hookbait to drift under the tree because I thought the fish would be snagged before I could get control if I did have a take. I decided to extend the tree instead. I snipped off a small branch end and taped two pieces of Biro tube along its stem. The line was threaded through and stopped near the hook. The whole lot was then lowered into the water and allowed to rest against the overhanging branches.

The choice of rig must be dictated by the conditions on the day. Fish on different waters react differently. On some waters line on the surface scares fish; on others they accept it. It is impossible to generalise or give easy solutions. Read all you can about the methods other people have used, then modify them with your own ideas until you get it right.

Bait

The range of baits available for surface fishing is considerable. It ranges from traditional crust through various home-made floater cakes, boilies (boiled, grilled, baked, fried, microwaved, bought in a bag), pet foods, cereals and snacks.

I have a definite preference for multiple or particle floaters as they give me greater scope for variations of feed pattern. Again, the advantage of fishing on the surface is that you can see the reaction of the fish to the bait you are offering them, so don't restrict yourself to Munchies or Mixers. Never visit a pet food store or a supermarket without assessing the wares for foods that would make a good floater. Then it's back to the kitchen sink with the new item. For starters, does it float? Then, how long does it take to soften? Will it take a hook, will it catapult out, will it take a colour, will it take a flavour? Some of my favourite recipes are given at the end of this chapter.

Watercraft

The carp angler who thinks that watercraft is something you hire on the Norfolk Broads, or that locating fish is only possible with the binoculars set at infinity, will not have experienced the tangle of emotions that the stalking carp angler goes through. Watercraft is such a personal thing that it's perhaps best explained by continuing the trip I was on at the start of this chapter.

When I arrive at the water it's the start of a familiar but still exciting routine. At least I managed the rest of that journey without going into a trance again; I could even remember some parts of the journey. There followed the ritual polishing of the polaroids. The small rucksack loaded with bait, catty, box of rig bits, controllers and so on hung on one shoulder. Rod, reel, spare spools (usually 6, 9, 12 and 18lb BS), landing net, sack and a couple of rod rests complete the wanderer's set-up.

Time to go walk about. Let's look at the open water first. What's the wind direction? Light south-westerly. Right, I'll start walking round towards the north-east margins; there are some high banks at that end of the lake, and I would also expect the fish to have drifted there on the wind. Slowly does it – a gentle stroll, trying not to miss anything.

Check the margin weeds on the way. Stand still, get used to the gentle sway of the reeds. Are any moving 'differently'? Any sudden vibrations or shaking as a carp glides through? No. Keep moving, then. Must not ignore these overhanging trees. Carefully put the gear down. Edge through the branches, trying to walk on eggshells. How come standing on a small twig can produce a sound like a rifle shot? Rambo never had these problems. Lean out through the branches and gaze down. Two fish, both upper doubles. How can they hang in the water so apparently motionless, so much masters of their environment? Store the information away and continue walking.

These lily pads are always worth a look. They seem dense but underneath it's relatively clear. Once again, slowly lower the gear and settle down to watch. Concentrate. Is that lily leaf moving more than little roach can move it? Yes! A line of leaves move and vibrate as an unseen force beneath parts the stems as it moves amongst the roots. How many? Just one, or more? Difficult to say. Move on, filing the information with the rest.

About halfway round, and it's time to catapult some baits into the open water. They should arrive in the margins further round at about the same time as I do. I've arrived in the corner but I've misjudged the speed of the drift and my baits have not arrived yet. I'll get as high as I can and see what's happening. Great, about two rod-lengths off the margin there are several fish just subsurface, the dark shapes moving in apparently random patterns.

What of my baits? The first ones are just drifting over the fish now. They are totally ignored. That's OK at this stage; all I'm concerned about is that the fish have not been spooked. Keep watching. Was that a flat spot in the ripples? That fish had a good look; the bait's still there but that swirl underneath is a start. Most of my free baits have gone over the fish now. Do I wait to see if the fish come right into the margin or what? The signs are that I've got to create more interest so it's back to the point where I first fired the bait in. This time I'll stay there for a good while and try to keep a steady stream of baits going in.

Right, time for another look. I've been feeding the middle for about an hour – not heavy feeding but a steady stream – and I know that even from where I'm sitting things have started to get interesting. Odd flat spots appear in the ripple, the occasional graceful back breaks surface. How am I going to fish this? I've got five, possibly six fish having a picnic. They seem confident enough but there's a build-up of missed bait at my feet. A few moments ago I noticed a pair of fish slowly glide past about a foot off the margins. They didn't take a bait but they knew they were there. What alternatives have I got? I could try to match the drift of those baits in the open water, the big advantage being that the fish are already feeding there. The disadvantage is that several baits are being missed by the fish, so I might have to recast several times, with the possibility of scaring fish before I get a take.

I could use an anchored bait, but I don't like the idea of a stationary bait in open water when all the other baits are moving. In addition I would have problems in casting it into position without scaring the fish.

Think again – any more ideas? What will happen when the

loose feed dries up? Experience suggests one of two things. They will continue to look where they are feeding now, but gradually lose interest in the search, or they will get fed up with waiting and go looking for more. In the latter case I've got a chance if I have a hookbait in amongst these free offerings.

First things first. Round to the side again to fire in some more free offerings to give me time to get organised. How am I going to do this? Slightly to my left is a dense bed of reeds. I can stand back in them, giving good cover, and I'll be able to see through to the hookbait. Any particular snags around? No, nothing special, so 12lb line should do fine, with a small branch controller, stopped about 2 feet from the hook. The controller can be deliberately snagged with the outer margin weed. This will stop the bait drifting too far into the weed and will easily strike out at the magic moment. Landing net assembled and hidden behind me. Rod rests? Better not. They would be nice but I daren't go close enough to the edge to put them in. Oh well, another stiff arm, but it's all in a good cause.

Ready, here we go. Where are the fish now? I can only see two. Wait a moment just to be sure. I'm glad I did that; I would definitely have spooked the one that just glided past in front of me. Right, slowly into position, one step at a time. Pause between each step. No signs of agitation, no bow waves – magic.

I've made it. I'm nearly surrounded by reeds, but have a clear view to the front. Bait on, gentle cast to my right and allow the controller to drift back to catch on the edge of the weed. Now then, breeze, swing my hookbait round to rest next to those free offerings. Good, nothing else to do now but watch and wait.

The last of the free offerings are drifting over the fish now. One turns and slowly, carefully, closes in on a small group of baits. Its head breaks surface as it sucks first one then two baits in before gently sinking back subsurface, to hang motionless as a tiny stream of bubbles escapes from its gills. I watch it for a little longer then it slowly moves out of sight to my left.

Anything moving in the margins yet? Nothing. I've been standing in this reedbed for about an hour and I'm having second thoughts. Not only does my arm ache, and my neck ache, and my back ache, but – more important – I've not seen any fish for a while. Have I got it wrong? If they've moved out of this corner where have they gone, and why? I'm sure I'm well hidden. Should I go round and fire more baits out, or wait? Everything looks right; I've got to wait; there's plenty of time yet.

Now that's more like it. Two fish, about a yard out. I didn't see them arrive but they're there now and that's all that matters. I'm sure they're interested in the baits. I can't explain it but I can almost sense and see their interest.

One turns to face the margin and starts to move in, nudging the second into movement as it does so. Both fish are now up against the margin weed and I can see the pectoral fins pivot as first one fish, then the other, tilts up to start sucking in the soft and bloated floaters. All aches are forgotten; I glance quickly down at my reel to make sure there are no loose coils of line. Must try to keep the rod end still – not easy the way my heart's thumping.

Now what? They've stopped for the moment. That's quite common; they often seem to feed in bursts of activity then drift off for a rest. They'll be back. Here they are. Well, I say 'they'; I can only see one but I'm sure the other will not be far off.

From where I was standing I could see every minute detail – the mouth opening and extending, the tiny whirlpool as another Mixer disappeared. Nothing else existed – time stood still. Only this tiny corner of the pond mattered. My own bait was next in line. Any second . . . now!

I've relived the trip many times. Every detail is sharply etched, a perfectly recorded mental video to be replayed at will – not just at traffic lights, but at any time the mind desires.

Commitment, patience and versatility – consistent surface fishing requires them all. It's hard work but the rewards can be great, not necessarily just in numbers of doubles or twenties, but in memories as well. I know of no other aspect of carp fishing that can involve me so completely. Sometimes I feel I've got it right; at others it's back to the drawing board. And I know that when it comes to the crunch I'm still only scratching the surface.

Bait Recipes

Floater Cake

I often use floater cake in conjunction with floating particles, loose-feeding particles but using floater cake on the hook. I find it particularly effective during the hours of darkness. My favourite recipe is as follows:

2oz casein	1oz fructose
3oz soya flour	1oz gluten
1oz sodium caseinate	½oz Vitmin
2oz wholewheat flour	

Cooking instructions:
1   Throughly mix the dry ingredients.
2   In a medium mixing bowl beat four eggs, plus required colour and flavour.
3   Gradually add dry ingredients, stirring well to produce a smooth, thick soup. NB You will not need all the dry mix for four eggs.
4   Line a shallow baking tin with foil and grease thoroughly (a 4-egg mix just fills a tray of 7 x 7 inches).
5   Pour in mix to a depth of approx ½inch.
6   Allow ten minutes for the mix to settle.
7   Cook in preheated oven at 375° F (190° C or gas 5) for 30 minutes. Timing is approximate and you might need to check regularly after 20 minutes.
8   Allow to cool, peel off foil.

Fried Floaters

Frying boilies produces a superb surface bait. My favourite version is made using Geoff Kemp's Protein Mix, but any good boiled bait mix will work.

1   Make the boilies as per instructions (try Geoff's Strawberry or Mellow Brandy flavour).
2   Prepare the cooking oil. I use a small non-stick saucepan with a fine metal strainer as my miniature version of a chip frier. (The hard part is getting the temperature right. I test with one bait; when hot enough, remove the pan from the heat and fry the rest of the baits; if you don't remove from the heat the baits burn very easily.)
3   After the baits have been fried, dry them on a kitchen towel to remove surplus oil.

Softening Cat and Dog Biscuits

Many of the cat and dog biscuits are hard and crisp when bought. Before use I prefer to soften them. This seems to give a better release of smell/flavour, as well as making hooking much easier. The problem is how to soften them without the biscuits soaking up too much water and becoming too soft. The following method works very well.

1 Half fill a suitable, sealable plastic box (size depends on the quantity required) with dry biscuits.
2 Cover biscuits with boiling water.
3 *Immediately* drain off the water
4 Seal the box then shake vigorously for several minutes (if you don't do this you'll end up with one giant bait).
5 Leave to cool, shaking occasionally.
6 Transfer to a plastic bag, seal and leave overnight.

You will find that by morning the biscuits look exactly the same as dry ones but have softened just enough to take a hook.

18

The Margins

On reflection I have caught a surprising number of carp from the margins. I don't need to be a psychologist to know what the average reader's reaction to that statement will be – 'That's all very well for him, he fishes private, secluded pools where there is no bankside pressure.' Well, here's the list of waters from which I've caught fish from the margins: Waveney D Lake, Cuttle Mill, Harlesthorpe Dam, Darenth Tip Lake, Snowberry Lake, Roman Lakes, The Tilery – in fact, a high percentage of the waters where I've caught carp.

Not all the margins I've caught from were under my feet, or even on the near bank, but many of them were. Carp visit the margins and they often feed there, so whenever you go to a water have a long, hard look at the banks and assess their potential for hotspots. Island and far-bank margins that are within casting distance tend to be pressured in angling terms but as a rule the near-bank margins aren't. It isn't my experience that carp are particularly scared of people in principle, they are more wary of them as a potential threat to their well-being. While they may not show close to the near bank during the day when there is a certain amount of movement, and the ritual socialising, when things are quiet they are just as likely to be in under the near bank as in the distant margins. Fishing under the rod tip or in unpressured areas of the near bank can bring great rewards. If fish aren't being caught in an area then they might well consider that area to be safe. The reject baits that you chuck into the water in front of you are very often taken by margin-patrolling carp, and you feel mighty proud of yourself the first time you lower an isolated hookbait to the foot of the near bank and then catch a carp on it. Apart from the satisfaction of such a capture there are few more exciting moments in all carp fishing than easing the hook into a carp that has taken off on a run from under your feet.

My first margin-caught carp was one of my earliest carp. I was fishing my first carp water, what was then the Robin Hood

One of my favourite fish: a margin – caught 24lb plus from Darenth Tip Lake, a pressured southern Leisure Sport water.

The brilliant Jim Fielding with a fine 20lb plus margin-caught fish. The water was gin clear and Jim able to watch the fish feeding on his baits.

pond in Loxley Valley, in the middle of a scorching hot afternoon. I was going through the motions really, but pleasantly so because I hadn't long been carp fishing and it was a lovely spot. I was float fishing tight to some lilies to my right when I noticed right at my feet a cloud of mud disturbed from the bottom. I was sitting close to the water on a basket and the mud cloud came up quite literally right at my feet. I reeled in gingerly, pressed some bread flake round the hook and lowered the bait into the mud cloud. The depth was all wrong and the float lay on its side. The exercise seemed a singularly pointless one – until the float set off across the surface towards the middle of the pond! It was a common carp, the dimensions of which would not impress the reader in the slightest, but which could well have been a personal best at the time at about six pounds.

The first time I really set my stall out to fish the near-bank margins was a few years later, at Snowberry Lake. I loved fishing the island margins at Snowberry but I wanted to get some confidence in particle fishing and picked Rod Hutchinson's brains on the subject. His advice was short, and to the point – 'Get 'em under the rod tip.' I don't think I was too convinced at the time. I spent the first two or three days of the next session studying the Snowberry margins. I still wasn't convinced. The water was fairly heavily fished at the time, which meant that there was a lot of bankside pressure, and I couldn't find a spot where the carp showed close to the bank. The more I thought about it the clearer it became that there was no angling pressure in the margins. I ruled out the shallowest margins, and the snaggiest because of the dangerous tree roots. In the end I decided on a corner pitch on the north bank. The

A bedraggled looking pair! A Tilery margin twenty hooked over a bed of tiger nuts during a rain-lashed, wind-blown, mud-encrusted session.

water was about four or five feet deep under my feet, there were bushes overhanging the water on either side of the swim, and there wasn't another swim for twenty or twenty-five yards in either direction. I fished the final day of the session in that swim, having introduced half a pan of maples the night before and another panful on the morning in question. Using three rods, I caught eight fish to 11lb plus, and they all took the left-hand bait – which was fished as tight to the bank as I could get it without actually having it in a bush. This was before the hair and I was using simple 6-inch bolt rigs with two maples on the shank of the hook.

On Waveney D Lake the far margins are pressured areas, but they still yield their share of fish. All the margins will produce fish but, again, the less pressured a bank is in angling terms the greater your chances may be. I have caught or seen fish caught from all the margins of D Lake, including a carp taken from under the rod tip in swim 3 in the middle of the day. This was an accidental capture, the angler concerned having reeled his baits in during a quiet period and dropped them under the rod tip! Needless to say, the near bank was far more heavily fished than the far bank for the rest of that day.

There is a great deal of casting out into the middle at Cuttle Mill, and I've done my share of it. In fact I like fishing the middle there because it is in that pressured area that the battle of wits between angler and carp is at its sharpest. One morning I drew peg 4. This used to be the end peg on the lawn (nearest the car park), and I didn't like the swim; it felt claustrophobic – because I couldn't cast out to the middle. I gave up on it and went across to the Long Pool, then had second thoughts and went back to the lawn. I now know that corner of the pool to be a productive one but I didn't at the time and was delighted to catch carp tight to the rushes, close to the rod tip. The next day I was fishing the middle bank, the swim opposite the end of the island. The fish were stacked up in front of the pontoon and the angler to my right didn't see why I should cast across him to get to the fish, so I sat and sulked. As I whiled away the blank and useless day I got to thinking about the fish of the day before. How did they get to that corner by the join of the lakes? As far as I knew there was no hotspot out in front of swim 4, or the first swim on the middle bank, so the patrol route didn't seem to be from the middle to the corner. Were they swimming along the margin under our feet? If they were they would be accustomed to finding discarded hookbaits. I tackled up a soft rod and dropped a bait a foot from the bank, and caught fish. Nothing very big, but it was action on a day when I was struggling and those are the days when any movement of the indicators is welcome.

I've had fish from both the near- and far-bank margins at Roman Lakes, and my friend Trevor Holland once had eleven carp in a day there on freelined maize – and you can't cast freelined maize very far. Harlesthorpe I rarely fished at a range greater than ten yards, and even then I found I was fishing over the fishes' heads on a number of occasions.

If many of my margin fish have been of distinctly average size then I think that is just a reflection of the waters they came from, and the fact that some of them date back some time. On the other hand, two of my better fish, which came from one of the most pressured waters in the country, Darenth Tip Lake, also fell to baits fished in the margin. These were carp of 26lb 10oz and 24lb 6oz and they came from the same spot, a quiet margin thirty yards down the bank from where I was fishing. My friend Nick Elliott caught a 30lb-plus margin fish from this same water during a February snowstorm! I would think that most carp men who don't know Darenth imagine that all the fishing there is at long range. It isn't; it's a water that rewards inventiveness and responds to change. The same can be said of many waters where the fishing has become stereotyped simply because the producing areas have become too heavily pressured and the anglers are ignoring the fact that unpressured areas have got to be explored.

One point about margin fishing. There is a temptation to create a baited area once you find you can catch fish from under the rod tip. It may pay off, but think about the situation before you do so. If the fish are unsuspicious of isolated baits don't risk

A quiet, unpressured water with hundreds of yards of undisturbed margins. This is a water I haven't had a true margin fish from! The natural feeding areas are well out from the bank, and that is where most of the fish are hooked.

alarming them by changing that situation. On some waters, at some times, baited areas create suspicion and you may spook otherwise catchable fish.

I started this chapter by saying that many people imagine that margin fishing succeeds only on quiet, secluded waters, or against distant or island margins. If you feel like that have a good look at your own water by studying the opposite bank and you may find unpressured areas that could produce fish.

In all honesty, I think that this look back at my own marginal experiences has surprised me, because I prefer to fish at long range – mainly because there is a great deal of bankside activity on many of the waters I fish. I guess I'll have to think it out again. The odd thing is that the one water I do fish that I could describe as quiet and secluded has not yet produced a margin fish for me. I think that's mainly because it's a natural water where the margins aren't looked on as a food source. It all goes to show how impossible it is to categorise waters.

19

A Fish from the Past

by Greg Fletcher

Redmire Pool – how many times have those romantic words been responsible for conjuring up visions of a far-off place, secluded and unapproachable, the home of giant fish of unbelievable cunning, its exact location a closely guarded secret?

All good, gripping stuff, eh? But that's exactly how it felt to me for many years. Then all the years of mystery were wiped away and I was there, on the bank with a week's fishing in front of me, in company with my friend Baz Griffiths.

My impressions of the place were mixed, really. One thing that does strike you instantly is how small the pool actually is. Nestling quietly in the Hereford border hills, you would hardly give it a second glance let alone believe that there were fish there. But we all know different – forty-odd twenties backed up by a good head of double-figures commons. This little water's ability to support such a head and weight of fish is staggering. But for all its apparent insignificance the pool undoubtedly has charm, character, unbelievable solitude and a definite charisma.

I started off in the Stumps while Baz, like myself a Redmire buff, wanted to spend his first night at Redmire at the scene of Walker's great triumph – in the Willow Pitch. We were on the water for the second week of the season; opening week had seen one twenty-pounder falling to Malcolm Winkworth. The weather had been lousy, with intermittent rain finding its way into the pool from the surrounding fields. This immediately ruled out one of the things we had both been looking forward to, which was spotting fish, especially on the shallows. The pool was like milky tea and fish could be seen only when they took to cruising just below the surface. Great fish they looked, too – mirrors, leathers and cracking commons, all good twenties. Other fish showed themselves – doubles, mostly commons, and a whole stack of little scamps around the 2lb mark.

All in all it was just nice to be there. What about the fishing?

An unusual view of the corner of the dam and oaks area at Redmire Pool.

Boilies generally had the indicators moving a couple of times a day, usually early morning. The best fish went 15lb and got me out of the bag at one in the morning – the only bite I had in darkness. Apart from an eight-pounder, all the other fish were scamp commons of about 2lb, all like peas in a pod and bright as a new penny.

A bait cast almost anywhere from the Stumps would produce a bite – margins, centre channel, far bank, it didn't seem to matter. One particular spot I found was way down the margins to my right. It was an easy cast for a left-hander, but being right-handed meant that I had to start a farcical cack-handed casting performance about tea time in order to give the swim time to settle down after the constant casting, pulling for breaks, retying, tangles and abortive chucks which could be expected before I finally got a bait a foot from the trailing branches. A yard or two further out and no bites – it was as simple as that.

I flogged away in the Stumps for half a week. Having lost a fish on the first night in the Willow Pitch, Baz had by this time decided to try his arm in the Evening Pitch. At this stage of the week our attitudes were definitely changing. At first it was a question of catching a Redmire carp, but now I made no bones about it – I wanted one of those twenties and had just three days left to get one. I spent the following day up trees desperately searching for clues as to where – or how – the bigger fish fed.

Because of the rain we were having the pool was still very coloured. No sooner did the rain ease up and the water start to fine down than the heavens would open up again for half a day and we would be back to square one – with zero water visibility. Most of the plans had to be made blind, so to speak. I couldn't accept that those bigger fish weren't feeding *somewhere* out there. They had to be, and I couldn't believe that with all the different spots I had cast to so far during the week the bigger fish hadn't come across the baits at some stage. Quite simply it boiled down to the fact that whatever I had been doing up to that time was not going to get me that twenty. In addition, the hotspot just off the branches down the margins definitely seemed cold as far as the bigger fish were concerned. I gave it one more night in the Stumps, with no action – not even from scamps. Next morning a move was definitely on the cards, but to where?

Baz was by now installed, somewhat uncomfortably, on the platform on the islands, so it seemed that with the dam end having had a rest for a couple of days the Willow had to be favourite. I moved there.

The weed directly in front of the swim, while not being impenetrable, was certainly thick enough to cause problems. It grew right to the surface and extended about ten yards out into the lake. Landing a fish was bound to be a problem and just setting the rods up was a headache. In the end the set-up I used was more suited to codding off Brighton Pier than carp fishing on one of the country's premier carp waters. Rods were stuck straight up in the air with the buzzers at shoulder height and the back rests set at three feet. I used no indicators or bobbins and the lines were kept as tight as banjo strings, fairly twanging out across the pool, to keep the line clear of the heavy weed.

The baits were our tried and tested boilies flavoured with a special banana flavour. The bait had never let us down and had caught carp the length and breadth of the country – in fact everywhere it had been used. So that surely wasn't a problem: these fish had never seen it before the start of that week. Earlier in the session it had been a case of using a couple of pounds of seeds with a single hookbait, a pop-up or a stringer fished over the top. I had almost used up all the hemp and tares I'd taken but there was still plenty of dari seed in the car. I'd hardly used it, apart from a few pouchfuls.

That was it then – all set in the Willow for the last two nights, dari out and single baits cast across to the Oaks directly opposite, with no action at all except for the eels just after dark. Recast at first light – still nothing. The swim seemed dead. (I mention this recasting because earlier in the week we had been leaving the overnight hookbait in position until later in the morning to avoid disturbing the swim. Looking back, I now think that this is a mistake at Redmire because of the eels, but we can all be wise after the event, can't we?)

That next-to-last night had seen the usual couple of pounds or so of seeds scattered around the area just off the branches of the Oaks and in front of the Outfall. With one night left something drastic was called for. There was probably thirty pounds of dari seed still in the motor – so out with the punt and the whole lot went over the side in the Oaks area with the three single hookbaits cast smack in the thick of it. Lines were jammed in the butt clips to keep them clear of the weed. Kettle on, a bowl of St Bruno and time to sit back and reflect on what I'd just done.

I was sure that fish would come in over the seeds, just as I was equally sure that they had been doing so all week. Perhaps with the swim saturated with dari, instead of a couple of pounds, it would hold the fish long enough for them to forget their natural caution and drop their guard. Maybe – and it was a big 'maybe' – they would stay around long enough to make a mistake with a hookbait.

So, with the trap set, there was nothing left to do but cook a meal, get in the bag and hope that the last night would bring something. I set the alarm for four o'clock and dawn saw me creeping along the dam looking for signs of activity. There was nothing whatsoever; in fact the swim looked completely barren.

I gave it until 6.30 a.m. then recast the left and middle rods back out over the seeds, which I was sure were still out there. In

Fletch with a couple of Redmire scamps.

153

a moment of madness I retied the right-hand rod with a 6-inch hooklink and the biggest pop-up I had left, which was about the size of a 2p piece. A further couple of minutes were spent balancing it with shot so it was only just held down. It looked ridiculous but the idea was that the bait would sit two inches off the bottom; if a fish so much as breathed it into its mouth the four inches of hooklength left behind the shot would quickly tighten up against the 2oz fixed lead sufficiently to nick the point of the hook in. So much for the theory side of things! All we needed was a fish to do its bit and complete the equation – but time was running out.

By now the sun was well up and sleeping was out of the question. Jack Hilton's book was in the back of the bivvy so I decided to spend an hour or two with Jack, Bill, Roger and the rest of the lads back in the late sixties until it was time to break camp and head back up north.

I was all wrapped up in the book and Jack had just landed his 'first of a run of leathers from Redmire Pool' when I heard one of the lines pluck out of the clip, followed immediately by the buzzer disturbing the peace and quiet. It was the right-hand rod cast at the outfall. The line was fluttering up through the rings and snaking out over the weed that choked the front of the swim. Jack and his pals were thrown heaven knows where – along with everything else between me and the rods! With the rods set so high it was a simple job to knock the bail arm in and wait for the line to tighten to the rod tip. What was in fact a few seconds seemed like an hour until the tip finally started to dip towards the Outfall. My overenthusiastic strike out of the rests was checked halfway back by something solid out there still sulking by the corner of the dam.

No scamp this one. No frantic jangling on the rod end, just a steady pressure and the odd heavy thump coming down into the palm of my hand. As soon as I'd hooked the fish I'd called Baz but he'd heard the Optonic and was halfway down the bank before I'd uttered a word. Because of the thick weed in front of the swim we'd decided it would have to be a boat job if I hooked anything. Baz arrived in seconds and made his way past the back of the bivvy and, without breaking stride, vaulted the stile and was heading across the dam for the punt.

The fish couldn't wait for our planned dramatics, though, and after a few more lunges in the centre channel shot for the thick weed in the corner of the dam to my right. My worst fears were about to be realised as it neared the weed. Keeping a tight line on it was only helping it towards sanctuary. It was muck or nettles time. If it was going to get into that stuff, better it did it

*Pete Springate was fortunate enough to capture Raspberry in 1983
and here he carefully returns this fine fish which is known to be more
than fifty years old.*

on top than deep down out of sight. It was a case of pumping like a lunatic – and up he came, swirling on top. For a few seconds everything was solid, but steady pressure got the whole thing on the move. In less time than it takes to tell, the fish, by now completely wrapped in weed, let itself be towed unceremoniously to the net without a murmur. The entire thing from start to finish took no more than three or four minutes and was over before the punt could arrive.

Baz paddled the punt back to the dam and joined me in the back of the swim. I'd been speculating on the weight of the fish while it was in the net – which was difficult with half a weedbed in there to keep it company!

As I cleared the weed away a big orange flank appeared. At first I thought it was the 'old Nude leather', but with more weed out of the way three scales appeared on the left flank. I recognised the fish straight away then. I had caught Raspberry, an old campaigner well known to Redmire regulars and caught many times down the years. Years, that was a thought. How many years had it been there? We did some quick sums and decided that, give or take a year or two, the fish was probably older than either of us.

The hook took some getting out and was well embedded in the middle of the bottom lip about one inch inside the mouth – the rig had worked a treat. A careful weighing gave us a weight of 24½ lb. The fish was in fabulous condition and despite its reputed age actually looked about five years old.

This was the very same fish that Jack Hilton had caught some fifteen years earlier and had referred to in his book as the 'first of a run of leathers from Redmire Pool'. It would be nice to think that it was going to be the first of many Redmire fish for me – but perhaps not. That fish meant a lot and to add to it a list of others would take the edge off it. No, it's best that that fish remains one on its own – though one of those big commons would be nice!

20

Session

I don't know how typical a session the chapter that follows represents. I had decided to write about it for the book in advance of the trip – whatever the outcome. If it isn't exactly representative of your carp fishing then you can treat it as an in-depth look at the outcome of addiction. You may also let it serve as a warning of what lies ahead if carp fishing really gets hold of you. The many who are already addicted will know that as sessions go this one is about par for the course.

I've just come back from a five-day session with my friend Bill Cottam. The water is private so I won't mention it, but it is a mere of 18 acres. It isn't a hard water, but it isn't an easy one either. You go there half knowing that the fishing will be slow going. If you really get it right, and the fish are in a co-operative mood, you can hope for two or three fish in five days. On the other hand, when the water is off you may struggle to hook a fish.

I've shown an inventory of the tackle and equipment I took with me. I think I'll keep this as a check-list because I'm always forgetting things. Twice I've set off without rods, and this time I forgot to take a cup (far more serious). By way of bait Bill and I took 10 kilos of hemp, 5 kilos of tiger nuts and 5 kilos of white dari seed. I took five 22-ounce mixes (dry weight) of paste particle, prepared and frozen up for storage in a friend's freezer for collection each day. My mix was slightly experimental and I wasn't at all sure of the level of the attractor I was trying out. Bill took two frozen mixes and six dry mixes for making up on the bank; he was fishing a tried and tested high nutritional value base mix fished in conjunction with a new attractor combination. (The experimental theme is because we sell bait and bait additives and we are always having to try things out.)

We arrived at the lake in mid-afternoon. Steve Allcott was the only angler on the water and he reported that the fishing was very slow. There had been two fish out in ten days – an eight pounder and a twelve-pounder. Well, the fish weren't

Ready for the off: the mountain of gear assembled for the five-day session.

being hammered, which was good news, but it didn't sound as though they were feeding on baits either, which was bad news. The water is a very natural one and at times the level of natural food available is such that these fish can afford to ignore baits, however good they are. It was wet and windy and as a rule the water does fish in those conditions.

I didn't feel that my bait was well enough established for me to fish any of the best-producing, most heavily pressured areas, so I opted for a little swim at the west end of the lake. 'Swim' is a bit optimistic; it's an area of mud made half-fishable by the addition of a few pallets. I got muddy setting up and stayed muddy for the rest of the five days – apart from during brief shopping trips.

Bill chose to fish one of the main producing swims, one that he hadn't fished before but which I was fairly familiar with. It was comparatively comfortable, which isn't a consideration either of us apply to swim selection, but I felt that catching from the pressured areas was likely to be hard work when the water wasn't really fishing. Unless I'm really on top of what I'm doing I feel that the known pressured areas from which the carp are caught with any sort of regularity may not produce for me. It is in these areas that you have got to have some sort of edge in terms of bait, bait application or presentation. The carp might not visit the less popular areas as often as the main ones but they can be more catchable there simply because they don't associate that area with danger.

Session Equipment Inventory

Tackle Box	**Tackle Bag**
Hooks of various sizes and types	Reels
Swivels	Buzzers
Drennan rings	Sacks
Beads, small and large	Scales
Bombs of various weights and types	Weigh-sling
	Barnett Diablo Slingshot
Braided line for hooklengths, 4 types	Drennan Feederpult
	Markers
Anti-tangle tubing	
Hair stops	**Equipment**
Superglue	Umbrella
Indicators	Storm sides or bivvy
PVA	Rod holdall
Cork and polystyrene	Bed-chair
Scissors	Bank sticks
Forceps	Indicator needles
Floater controllers	Landing net
Tape	Rods
Torch	Camera Equipment
Spare catapult elastics	Waterproofs
Aquarium tubing	Change of clothing
Small hacksaw (!)	Sleeping bag
Polaroids	Foam mattress
	Cushion for pillow
	Warm clothing for nights

We got very wet setting up but were fishing by the middle of the evening. There is a boat on the water which is used for all the groundbaiting. I don't like boats and carp fishing – I think they give the angler too much assistance; bait application is too easy, which means that it tends to be overdone. Artificial feeding grounds are easily created at range and it is soon difficult to come up with any sort of surprise element through inventiveness, or graft. I carry three different types of bait dropper with me for feeding at range, but on this particular water everyone else uses the boat, so when in Rome . . . . There would be a slower accumulation of pressure on the water if the boat wasn't used, though.

We were fishing to markers, using the boiled baits over the top of tiger nuts and/or seeds. We wanted the fish preoccupied when they encountered the hookbait to increase the chances of them making a mistake and getting hooked, but as the water was 'off' we weren't at all sure of the quantities of bait we should use. We didn't want too great an accumulation of feed in the swim, but I think this problem may have been largely in the mind. Seeds aren't a problem in this respect: even if the carp don't get their heads down the small fish in the water clear the seeds. On that water there is no accumulation of boiled baits, either. There is a large head of eels present and their selection of paste baits appears to be less discriminating than that of the carp; the eels will eat anything and on some nights can be a real menace. We were using tiger nuts because they stay in the swim until the carp eat them (they don't go off) and indications were that the carp were still feeding on them – in the fourth season of their use. Of the seeds, I was using hemp and Bill was using white dari.

I had some reservations about the groundbaiting situation for a number of reasons.

1.   If the carp weren't really feeding, a heavily baited swim would be meaningless.
2.   It was more than possible that the carp were starting to shy away from baited areas.
3.   Although some carp were still taking tigers, others could be spooking off them. This consideration could also apply to the hemp, but wasn't likely to in the case of the white dari as only Bill and I had used it on the water.

Not the safest of casting platforms!

160

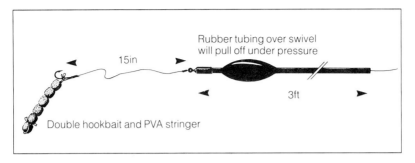

Initial presentation.

4.   Small fish are very active over seeds. While this may draw carp to the feeding area initially, in time they may start to associate danger with the small-fish activity. The smaller fish can also draw the predatory eels into the swim.

I wasn't sure about the level of the main attractor in the paste particle I was using, either. I'd tried it at ⅓ millilitre on the previous session, with no apparent reaction from the carp. For this session I was using five drops of the attractor in a 22oz mix, but it still smelt a bit strong. I refer to the bait as a paste particle because it was chopped up small, producing 800–1000 baits per mix.

I rowed the markers out and put the groundbait down. Bill opted for a big bed of baits to keep the feeding fish, if any, moving round the swim. I fish that way when I'm using biggish boiled baits over groundbait and feel that the carp are feeding well, but on this occasion I decided to keep the baited area as small as possible. If a carp did come in to feed I wanted it to have the best possible chance of finding the hookbait, which I was fishing in conjunction with a PVA stringer close to the edge of the groundbait area. With this type of fishing you are gradually concentrating the carp's attention on to the hookbait without making it aware that you are doing so. You're trying to distract, or preoccupy, the fish to the extent that it will forget the possible danger and make a mistake. Theory and practice can be two very different things so you have to keep reassessing the situation as you go along.

Hookbait presentation we had to feel our way in on, taking some account of the methods we thought, or knew, had been in use on the water. It might just be that the fish weren't coming out because they had wised up to the presentations in use. I kept it as simple as possible to start with – small double baits fished

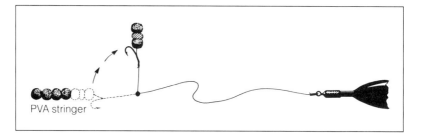

Suspended baits rise up as the PVA dissolves.

tight on the bottom and cast out with a six-bait stringer. Hooklength started at 15 inches; hooks were size 8 Lion d'Or strong-wire spade-ends whipped to 12lb BS Masterbraid by means of the Domhoff knot; main line was 11lb Sylcast. Heavy gear, but the margins are very snaggy and there was a real danger of the fish kiting into the lily pads to my right. I fished over one bed of bait the first night, fishing a hookbait on each side in the hope of trapping a fish on the way into, or out of, the baited area. Sticking to the edges means that there is less chance of the main line spooking a feeding fish, although the total absence of line bite activity on the water, even over a concentrated hemp bed, gives a clear indication of just how aware the fish are of the tackle. On the third rod I fished a double-bait PVA stringer set-up, well away from the baited area with no free offerings round it.

There was no indicator action on the lake during Sunday night although conditions seemed ideal. As a general rule the water only fishes at night or in the early morning. Steve pulled off on the Monday. He felt that chances would be better at Savay in the very windy conditions. Bill and I had four nights left on the water and we were very hopeful. During Monday afternoon Bill moved into the swim Steve had vacated, which meant that we were fishing the same general area of the water.

We both fished suspended baits the second night and I switched to size 6 Lion d'Or spade-ends. Fishing balanced or buoyant baits means that you can get away with a heavier, stronger hook. I also changed my groundbaiting pattern, fishing two baited areas instead of one. I wanted one area without hemp to cut down on small fish activity, using just tiger nuts and the paste particle as groundbait. The hemp marker was at about 50 yards and the second marker further right, at roughly 70 yards.

The fishing was hard. Bill had a real struggle of a week, which made a change because he usually outfishes me on the

Home for five days on a sea of mud.

water. Things weren't made any easier for him when he had to change his bait halfway through the week. We agreed that his original smell level was too high, which meant that he had to try and establish a bait with a new smell in one of the most pressured areas at a time when the carp didn't want to know anyway. I was more fortunate in that I did have some activity.

I think I had a near miss on the Monday night. There was a sharp buzz from one of the alarms in the early hours. I looked out across the calm surface and saw a heavy swirl over the baited area, presumably from a fish spooking off the hookbait. Presentation was a problem. There was no other action that night.

I concentrated my groundbaiting more and more as the week went by in the hope that however short a time a fish spent over the baits it was at least likely to encounter the stringer, and the attendant hookbait.

Tuesday night was wet and wild but there was no action through the hours of darkness. On Wednesday morning I was up soon after first light; it was becoming a struggle and I needed that first cup of coffee of the morning to put my mind back together. Expectation builds up through the day on a night-feeding water, but when the night turns out to be blank you

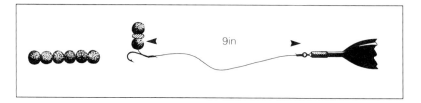

A double hookbait balanced with cork to just sink – held down by the weight of the hook alone.

have to adjust to the realisation that you have another fifteen or eighteen hours to get through before you can start expecting action again. Mentally I was handling the session well and that morning I was already adjusted to the continuing blank when I was away on the middle rod – the left-hand rod of the far marker.

A run! An absolute flier. I squelched to the rods, knocked the bail arm in, watched the line start to tighten up on the water – running straight out, no liner – and pulled back hard on the rod. I felt no pressure; the line didn't even start to lift from the water before it parted some twenty yards beyond the rod tip. I felt sick and reeled in to examine the end of the line, knowing what had happened. The line was badly frayed for some distance and heavily scored at the point of breakage. I knew a pike must be responsible but didn't know if I'd had a run and had then been bitten off by a pike striking at the moving line, or if the initial run had come from a pike accidentally grabbing the line as it chased prey close in. At the time I thought that the latter theory was correct and didn't feel bad about the 'loss'. Later events suggested that it was a run and that the pike had struck at the moving line. Either way I'd had a moment of high hope, and had then been dropped back to rock bottom when no fish had resulted. I was quite sure the 11lb BS Sylcast was in perfect condition when I cast out. (Later Bill had a couple of unexplained occurrences which could have been caused by a fish trailing line; I couldn't find the lost end tackle and 50 yards of line in the swim; Fletch and Bill retrieved the lost end tackle and line – minus the semi-fixed lead, I'm glad to say – from the pads during the following session.)

The possible run had come to a suspended bait fished an inch off the bottom. I wasn't too happy with the presentation and for the last two nights I switched from suspended to balanced baits, still fished in conjunction with stringers, using cork to achieve neutral buoyancy of the two small baits. That fine carp angler John Lilley had first shown me this presentation and I

*The precarious rod set up. I'm fishing butt clipped with a heavy
Micky Sly indicator to register any movement, including drop backs.*

liked it very much. I was still having problems rationalising what the carp were doing when confronted by a suspicious bait, presuming that the problem was one of presentation. They weren't confident enough to make a mistake with the hookbait through preoccupation because they weren't feeding heavily enough – and because the bait wasn't well enough established.

As the week wore on I felt that their confidence in the baited areas might increase, and there had been some action to justify that belief. If they became really preoccupied I could fish a short hooklength with the baits tight to the bottom, but at that stage I thought I was probably at halfway house. Confidence in the bait would be increasing, but not to the extent of preoccupation. I was still fishing for a momentary indiscretion. I shortened the hooklength down to 9 inches and balanced the bait. If they were sucking at the baits these would pass a none-too-close examination. Time was too short to ring all the changes I wanted to try, to go through all the presentation permutations. I had to remember Dennis Davies's words, 'Once they want it enough they will take it on any sort of presentation', and hope that I was getting near the point where they were starting to want it enough. In reality there was very little difference between the suspended presentation I'd been using and the balanced one I finished up with, but eels are more of a nuisance with suspended baits.

I went across to Bill's swim during the morning but he was having a mental battle with the session. I knew the feeling and left him to sort himself out. I somehow contrived to fall in at some stage of the morning, but we'll not go into that, eh?

Wednesday brought two other anglers on to the water and they set up in the swims to Bill's left. I watched them apply their ground bait from the boat and a terrific amount of feed went in, covering a considerable area of the lake. They were consistently successful on the water and the amount of feed Bill and I were using seemed insignificant by comparison with theirs. Watching someone else starting a session can undermine your confidence, particularly when you aren't catching, and watching Roy applying his bait did raise doubts in my mind. They weren't rational doubts though, it was just the gnawing uncertainty of undermined confidence and the inevitable conviction that someone coming on to the water when you are struggling will catch!

Two more nights. On Wednesday night I was woken up by an eel of 2lb or so. I quite like eels but they do disturb the swim, and they are less than easy to unhook in knee-deep mud on a pitch-black night. We got on all right and I unhooked it and put

The reward for five days' 'hard work'. In the sack is the common of 18lb 8oz. The sack/sling is made by Joan Bagshaw of Sheffield and is the most supportive weighing sling I've come across.

it back. I rebaited, tied a fresh stringer and recast to the 70-yard marker. The cast felt and sounded right but it was starting to get light so I sat up drinking coffee, then repositioned the end tackle at first light. There was no further action and none elsewhere on the lake.

Another day, and the last night coming up. Out in the boat late afternoon or evening. I put the last 5lb of hemp in at the near marker, together with about ½lb of tiger nuts and a couple of handfuls of paste particles. A couple of pounds of tigers and a pound of paste particles went in at the far marker. Keep your mind intact. Keep doing what you think is right and hope for a result. No one was catching, which made it easier for me to believe in what I was doing – but I'd been using the bait for ten days by this time without taking a fish on it. If something was wrong with the bait it meant that everything I was doing was wrong, but it felt right in terms of the smell level, and the base mix I knew to be right.

Thursday night brought one quick lift to the right-hand isotope indicator in the early hours. I opened one eye, regretted the fact that the isotopes were out of line and went back to sleep. I was up soon after five and, over coffee, had the usual early-morning battles with myself. Were the baits still on, or had the eels nibbled them away? Should I reel in, rebait and recast? I decided not to disturb the swim and accept the blank with a good grace.

At ten to six I was away on the left-hand rod, the first sign of action of any sort from over the hemp bed. Keep going, keep going . . . I shut the bail arm, let the line tighten and lifted into the run. Everything went absolutely solid; nothing moved; it was almost as though I'd struck into a snag. The bait had been very close to the marker and I looked out to see if it was moving. No. I kept a steady pressure on and eased the rod tip up. Very slowly it started to move, and whatever was at the other end of the line moved with it.

For a while I thought it was another eel, but an anxious, unspectacular scrap brought an 18½lb common carp rolling into the net. It made me quite happy and after I'd sacked it I punched the air with *both* fists – two or three times!

End of session. I went hoping for something bigger, but it was the only fish out of the water while we were there and for once I came away from the lake thinking I'd fished it reasonably well. As long as you can keep your mind intact and work at what you are doing, I think that you learn far more from the hard sessions than you do from the ones when catching comes easy. As Dick Walker said, waiting can be very hard work –

particularly in a claustrophobic, muddy swim when the fish don't seem to be feeding.

Footnote: 'I went hoping for something bigger' does not imply that an 18½lb common is not a big fish. We were, quite literally, fishing for bigger fish on that water. We do fish other waters where a 14lb fish gives us enormous pleasure.

21

Carp Fishing Involvement

The carp world extends far beyond the banks of carp lakes. It represents a developing culture and has its own literature, meetings, conferences and organisations. There are three carp-fishing organisations, the Carp Society, the Carp Anglers Association and the British Carp Study Group. As I co-founded The Carp Society with my friend Greg Fletcher, and I'm currently editor of its publications *Carp Fisher* and *Cyprinews*, I can hardly claim to have a totally unbiased view of the respective merits of the organisations, or their publications. So if you would like to know more about Peter Mohan's groups I would suggest you write to him at Heywood House, Pill, Bristol, enclosing a stamped addressed envelope.

You can obtain information about the Carp Society by writing to the membership secretary, Vic Cranfield, 33 Covert Road, Hainault, Ilford, Essex. As it happens, most of the contributions to this book are by anglers with a heavy involvement with the Carp Society. Baz Griffiths is general secretary; Vic Cranfield membership secretary; Greg Fletcher conference secretary; Bill Cottam is a regional organiser for Yorkshire and magazine distributor; Brian Skoyles and Ken Townley are regional organisers for East Yorkshire and Devon and Cornwall respectively, and Brian Garner gives slide shows and laughs a lot ('Listen, I am the Kiddie'). Dave Preston is a one-off, writes for the society's magazine *Carp Fisher*, and is a tackle manufacturer and innovator.

Some carp anglers join organisations, others don't. You learn a great deal from an involvement with other carp men and I've always found the majority to be very friendly both on and off the bank, and very informative *off* the bank. (Never seek information on the bank, particularly from session men. We become different people when we are divorced from reality and trying to make a hit with carp that just don't want to know.) I'm sure you will benefit a great deal from membership of one

(a)

(b)

*The future is for them. Two Carp Society Under Sixteens
(a) Hadrian Frankland and (b) Ian Ashton from Huddersfield with
two of their carp from a Society fish-in.*

of the organisations. The publications are first class (the fact that I edit it modestly prevents me from admitting that *Carp Fisher* is universally acclaimed as the leading carp fishing/angling magazine in this country); there are numerous meetings on a regional basis and national conferences every year.

Tailpiece

Here are a few boring statistics. It took me thirty-three years and ten months to catch my first carp. It then took me a further five years to land my first double-figure carp, two more years to catch my first twenty and a further five years to catch a 30lb-plus fish. As I write, my first thirty is nearly five years into the past, which means that I am roughly seventeen years on from the capture of my first carp.

I have fished a great deal in the intervening years and have had good seasons and bad, both in terms of enjoyment and in terms of catching carp. At times I have been impatient to achieve whatever I was aiming for, but not often. It takes time to achieve anything, and you cannot hurry time, any more than you can slow it down. In carp fishing you have to treat time as being on your side or it will become your enemy. When I was younger a year seemed a long time; now it is nothing – and five years very little. If you want to be a carp fisher take your time. In the carp world 'success' is measured in terms of acceptance, not in figures, and you will achieve acceptance only when it is granted you by your fellow carp anglers. Most are accepted because they demand nothing. Others seek acclaim and are treated with suspicion. Take your time. If you catch a thirty with your first cast you will view it as an achievement; everyone else will know that it is luck. Five years on you will know that it was luck.

I know many people in the carp world; I meet them on the bank and at Carp Society meetings. They all have one thing in common, they are anglers – most of them carp anglers. In terms of catching carp some of these anglers are extremely successful, others less so, still others downright unsuccessful. Some I don't know about at all, even to the extent that I don't know whether they have caught a carp or not. Some are professional men, some tackle and bait dealers, some dustmen, many unemployed. A few are black, many white, one or two Welsh and Scottish, and there is Alf Romp from Slough. I've been meeting many of these fellow carp men over a number of years now. We

If it makes you feel like this you're doing it right! Steve Justice with a big common and a big smile.

meet, pass the time of day, rarely, if ever, discuss fish, have a drink and pass on into the next year, or five years, or whatever brief carp-fishing period will pass before our next meeting.

It is nice to catch, but what you catch will be a private triumph and may mean more to you than to the bloke down the bank who hasn't caught for half a lifetime. You will find that the nicer you are to other carp anglers the happier they will be for you when it is your turn to catch. But what our fellow carp men put on the bank matters not a jot to any of us in terms of acceptance. We know that we all share the same hopes, dreams, ambitions, trials and tribulations, disappointments, disasters – and occasional triumphs. Your success in carp fishing is measured by the pleasure you derive from it. All my fish successes have been very private at the time because they would have meant very little to anyone else anyway. For every single success there are a thousand disappointments in terms of catching fish, a fact that it pays to be mindful of in your relationships with other carp men. We all try not to let it show but there are times when other people's fish *hurt*. Smile through it all and determine to get it right next time.

You are a carp man from the moment you cast out your first bait . . . I think that is a sentence that can have no ending. Although people do give up carp fishing they still tend to be looked on as carp anglers. The late Dick Walker, BB, Dave Steuart, Jack Hilton – the list is endless. Carp men. They were involved with it and they felt it, as we do. Dick Walker is no longer with us and as far as I know BB, Dave Steuart and Jack Hilton no longer fish for carp, but they left the carp world a richer place for their passing through it. Enjoy being a carp man, wear the title with pride, and try to leave the carp world a richer place for your passing through it.

My grateful thanks to Brian Naylor, Greg Fletcher, Brian Garner, Bill Cottam, Dave Preston, Vic Cranfield, Brian Skoyles and Ken Townley for their considerable contributions to this book. I hope the richness of their experiences will help you in your carp fishing. When you read their tales again, appraise the manner of their achievement rather than the achievement itself.

Whatever you want from your carp fishing, I hope this book will help you enjoy achieving it – or achieve enjoying it.

Other fishing titles from The Crowood Press

Carp – The Quest for the Queen
John Bailey and Martyn Page   ISBN 0 946284 19 9

In Visible Waters   *John Bailey*   ISBN 0 946284 80 6

Pike – The Predator becomes the Prey
John Bailey and Martyn Page   ISBN 0 946284 47 4

Reflections from the Water's Edge
John Bailey   ISBN 1 85223 080 0

River Fishing   *Len Head*   ISBN 0 946284 71 7

Roach – The Gentle Giants
John Bailey   ISBN 1 85223 035 5

Stillwater Coarse Fishing
Melvyn Russ   ISBN 0 946284 83 0

Tench   *Len Head*   ISBN 0 946284 72 5